Neo-Classical Dramatic Criticism
1560–1770

# Neo-Classical Dramatic Criticism 1560-1770

THORA BURNLEY JONES

AND

BERNARD DE BEAR NICOL

CAMBRIDGE UNIVERSITY PRESS

CAMBRIDGE

LONDON · NEW YORK · MELBOURNE

Published by the Syndics of the Cambridge University Press
The Pitt Building, Trumpington Street, Cambridge CB2 1RP
Bentley House, 200 Euston Road, London NW1 2DB
32 East 57th Street, New York, NY 10022, USA
296 Beaconsfield Parade, Middle Park, Melbourne 3206, Australia

First published 1976

Printed in Great Britain
at the
University Printing House, Cambridge
(Euan Phillips, University Printer)

*Library of Congress Cataloguing in Publication Data*

Jones, Thora Burnley, 1919–

Neo-classical dramatic criticism, 1560–1770.

Bibliography: p.

Includes index.

1. Dramatic criticism – History.  2. Neoclassicism (Literature)
I. Nicol, Bernard de Bear.  II. Title.

PN1707.J6   809.2   75–16873
ISBN 0 521 20857 2 hard covers
ISBN 0 521 09971 4 paperback

# Contents

# Acknowledgments

The authors are indebted to Miss Mona McKay, Librarian of Loughborough College of Education, and her staff and to librarians throughout the country who willingly lent many scarce volumes, without access to which this book could never have been completed.

# I

# Introduction: Aristotle and Horace

Attitudes to neo-classical dramatic criticism have changed little since last century when it was fashionable to believe that the post-Renaissance critics endeavoured to perpetuate a doctrine of formalism which gave practitioners neither good guidance nor sound assumptions on which to base their work. The specimens selected for detailed examination in the following pages may throw a more liberal light on the criticism of this period. To take an example of the older view, it has been said that the doctrine of the unities provides a stultifying model, yet on reflection one may well ask whether this is necessarily so or always so. The moral purpose which neo-classical critics felt to be the very heart of serious drama is sometimes censured by those moderns who in the same breath make a case for 'committed' literature. The idea of mimesis in the Aristotelian sense is under attack in a manner apparently calculated to blur the line between life and art although it has not yet been clearly demonstrated that the line is not a matter of considerable importance. A passing glance at, say, Scaliger, may lead one to the hasty conclusion that this seemingly sapless grammarian has little of moment to record, but on looking more closely at these early critics, one quickly perceives that an earnest search is in progress for a theory of drama, based on principles first expounded by Aristotle, but tested, and in different degrees distorted by their application to very different theatres serving very different communities.

This kind of period study will in its nature reflect changes in social, economic and political contexts. We start from the assumptions of an aristocratic society and move into a world dominated by middle-class ambitions and implications of newly discovered entitlements. From Scaliger to Diderot is a journey from the post-Renaissance Italian court to the eighteenth-century drawing-room and on the personal level from a highly organised hierarchic public world to the private darkness and vexations of the individual soul. We become aware of the perils of passing judgment on a critical view when we may in fact merely be censuring a society towards which we have an ingrained antipathy. The isolation of a scale of dramatic values in a state of clinical purity is revealed for the absurdity which it is and each critical statement is seen to maintain its status only as a starting point for a discussion of its validity in a given context.

While the relativity and continued search for readjustment of value judgments with the consequent search for new analytical tools are revealed in this brief study, so too is the permanence, or apparent permanence, of certain critical approaches to drama. Aristotle isolated many problems about drama which seem to recur in every age whenever plays are critically examined. Sometimes the neo-classical critics misinterpreted the nature of Aristotle's questions or provided alternative answers based on non-Aristotelian reasoning. They approached the *Poetics* as if it were a treatise on rhetoric and manufactured a curious amalgam of pseudo-Aristotelian and Horatian precept. Nevertheless, they used the ancients as a starting point for the discussion of matters which seemed relevant to them in their time and which still lie at the heart of most works on drama published in this present age.

For instance, they considered the relationship between the fictional truth of the theatre and the reality of the world outside it, or, in neo-classical terms, 'veri-similitude' and 'truth', a complex relationship which both binds the play on the stage to the audience's experience of life outside it and at the same time separates it from that life. The actor who has been killed on the stage is not dead. Fiction, the description of events which have not happened, and reality or our interpretation of those events which we think have happened and are happening, are reconciled in the theatre and the process of reconciliation has puzzled most critics. An action has been imitated, but what is the relation of the imitation to the action? Castelvetro is never at ease in the world of illusion and comes down on the side of history, defined as a description of what he considers to have been real events; consequently he relegates drama to the lower status of a pastime suitable for those of feeble intellect. Contrariwise, Sidney elevates poetry, including drama, to a plane of ideality beyond nature, so that the truth of fiction authenticates itself by virtue of its freedom, not being shackled to a description of existential experience. In the writings of Diderot, we read how one man in a lifetime of reflection moved from the position of confusing life and dramatic action to an acceptance of the essential barrier between life, in so far as we are able to feel and respond to its random impact, and the composed narrative about possible lives, which is the art of drama or fiction.

These neo-classical critics are also concerned, as we are today, about the continuing relationship between drama and the social realities of its time.[1] Drama in the sense of statement achieved through theatrical devices seems to have developed out of religious ritual. Both in Greek and Greco-Roman drama and in post-Renaissance European

---

[1] This relationship is examined in detail by Elizabeth Burns in *Theatricality*.

drama, the line of development indicates a move from the exploitation of myth and symbol towards a more literal representation of life as it is experienced, a structured reflection of social modes and manners and of the responses of men and women to the social pressures and demands of their age. Elizabethan drama and to a less but still significant extent French classical drama are rooted in an authoritarian society of which inevitably authors, critics and audience are part. The later instability of an evolving society is reflected in the challenge to the hard prescriptive neo-classical line, a challenge which finds expression in the qualified formalism of Samuel Johnson and in the search for a 'popular' theatre described in the writings of Diderot and Mercier.

Apart from being an imitation of life, a mirror of customs and an image of truth, has drama any social function, any obligation to operate beyond itself, to feed back into the society which it reflects a pattern of behaviour, a model for a universally acceptable ethic or a codification of laudable social action? Aristotle appears to have answered in the negative, certainly as far as tragedy is concerned, but his commentators, as will be seen, came to many different conclusions. Horace gave a positive invitation to treat drama rhetorically, as doctrine, as a means of moving and improving an audience as well as entertaining them. Neo-classical critics, nurtured on the writings of medieval divines, of whom they felt themselves the true successors, preferred the Horatian position and this has come into fashion once again in the convictions of those committed authors and critics who maintain that social institutions must here and now be radically altered and that drama along with the other arts must play its part in helping the bad old world give birth to the brave new world.

Fourthly, our critics will declare their concern for the

4

nature of events within the theatre. In what manner is this imitation of an action being carried out and what kind of actions should be the subject of imitation? They are writing with one eye on the ancient doctrine and the other on the theatre of their own day, which was not medieval theatre where the actor in the morality tradition represented a good or bad quality, a human virtue or a vice. Sixteenth-century theatre, moving away from the pure morality towards something more concrete, more personalised, doubtless also more materialistic, encouraged questions about the kind of stories audiences liked to hear, and particularly about their readiness to listen to a tale of woe and misery. Towards the end of the period, in the mid-eighteenth century, discussion centres more and more on the resemblance of the character being acted on the stage to the person sitting in the auditorium. Shakespeare's characters, in Johnsonian criticism, are subjected to the test question: Is this how I would have felt and reacted in this situation? What is happening on the stage is now considered as a replica, exaggerated so as to conjure up laughter or pity, of what I imagine might be going on in my neighbour's house. Mimesis comes closer to mere copying, or, as it was later called, 'naturalism'. Sidney asks that the theatre illumine an ideal world; Mercier urges his poet to become acquainted with the abattoirs of Paris and the suburbs of Lyon.

There is constant reference, too, in these writings to what Professor Styan calls the elements of drama,[2] the terms of the convention which writers, actors and audience agree to accept. Aristotle listed six such elements: plot, character, diction, thought, spectacle and song. Should one play contain both tragic and comic incidents in its plot? Are some characters unsuitable for presentation on the stage or in certain kinds of plays? Is it

[2] J. L. Styan, *The Elements of Drama.*

5

acceptable or absurd for characters to speak in verse rather than in prose, and if verse, has blank verse certain attributes denied to rhymed verse or vice-versa? Neo-classical critics were unsure of the purpose and propriety of a chorus. Arrangement of the incidents is subjected by – for instance – D'Aubignac to a detailed analysis which shows that even if the earlier critics may have tried to write a grammar of the theatre and nearly suffocated it with theory, their immediate successors brought a considerable understanding of the essential nature of drama, its demands, its materials and its structure, to their scrutiny of 'the theatre in practice'. Following Donatus and Scaliger rather than Aristotle, the earlier critics had no doubts about their structural geometry. A play set off from a given starting point, explored the complexities of its plot in measured sequences and arrived at its destination in a manner which precluded a random choice of endings. The formula was sound, durable and sufficiently flexible to avoid obvious repetition of patterns, at least for a couple of centuries. If it is no longer valid in our time we are probably still searching for adequate substitutes. We may tamely accept the view that process has precedence over form, but if form disappears completely, process might find itself without a vehicle of communication, or at best with a vastly underpowered one.

Sufficient has been said to indicate that the matters raised by the critics of this period have more than mere historical interest, and that few topics of real and permanent importance to a discussion about drama have escaped their notice. They tend, it is true, to be cursory about the actor himself, his training, techniques and mental orientation towards his craft. We have to wait for Diderot, inspired by his admiration for Garrick, to provide a sustained and detailed meditation on the theory of acting. The historical explanation for this is simple and probably correct. Until Garrick (even allowing for Nell Gwynn) the actor tended to be looked on as a menial, of little account as a person, earning his precarious livelihood in the exercise of a craft which he picked up by practice. If he was successful, he was deemed to be so in virtue of his nature and there the matter ended. Johnson's relationship with Garrick as described by Boswell is typical. Talking of Garrick, he said: 'He is the first man in the world for spritely conversation'.³ or again, 'And after all, Madam, I thought him less to be envied on the stage than at the head of a table.'⁴ The matter of theatre architecture is a separate issue, already well documented, and no attempt has been made in the following pages to re-tread any of this ground.

Ideally, one would like to ask the reader to have a copy of Aristotle's *Poetics* in front of him, ready for immediate reference when the commentaries of the earlier neo-classical critics are under review. The following summary of Aristotle's main points is offered as an *aide-mémoire*.

He begins by pointing out that epic, tragedy, comedy, dithyramb, most flute music and harp music, are all forms of representation, or re-creations of reality. The desire to imitate, he says, seems to be inborn in men from childhood. One of these forms of imitation is called tragedy, which differs from epic in so far as epic is in narrative form and can cover an unlimited stretch of time. Tragedy usually tells a story the events of which take place in one revolution of the sun. This, it should be noted, is Aristotle's only reference to 'unity of time'. In his sixth chapter he comes to the heart of the matter with a definition of tragedy. Tragedy deals with the serious

³ J. Boswell, *Life of Samuel Johnson*, ed. Ingpen, p. 242.
⁴ Ibid. p. 1031.

7

concerns of living, is complete in itself (i.e. has a formal unity) and is of a certain length. The action is demonstrated in front of an audience, not narrated to them, and in the course of the performance the emotions of pity and fear are aroused and 'purged'. The exegeses centred on the concept of purging (catharsis) have through the ages reached almost theological proportions. Explanations have taken in general either an ethical, a psychological or an aesthetic turn. Our sixteenth- and seventeenth-century commentators, bringing Horace to their aid, adopted, as will be seen, the ethical view that catharsis, purging, means quite simply a moral cleansing. One becomes a better person for being acquainted with heroic suffering. The psychological view adopted by later generations of critics (we see it starting in Johnson) translates the language of moral philosophy into the language of neurology. Pent-up instincts and desires are allowed the free range of the imagination for a time and a profound human need is satisfied. The aesthetic argument, made explicit in noble terms by A. C. Bradley at the turn of the century, invokes the abstractions of sublimity, beauty, awe as the source of a special kind of pleasure. We delight in the knowledge that man can look down into the abyss of despair and still retain his humanity. Catharsis as a form of exaltation brought about through the blending of 'passion with enlightenment'[5] is yet another reading which might be taken as an attempt to combine the psychological and the aesthetic views.

Of the six parts of tragedy which Aristotle categorises, those which encouraged long and careful reflection on the part of later critics are plot and character. Why does he say that plot is the soul of tragedy and takes primacy over character? 'Plot' may be given a simple or a complex meaning and either, or both, would seem to fit Aristotle's

[5] John Gassner in *European Theories of Drama*, ed. Barrett H. Clark.

train of thought. If plot is taken to mean simply the arrangement of the incidents in the sense that the plot of *Hamlet* is the revealing of a series of happenings which culminate in the death of the king, and of course of Hamlet and others, then the plot patently comes before the characters. (References to playwrights' notes and letters are irrelevant here – e.g. Ibsen's story of sketching out *The Wild Duck* without characterisation or contrari-wise Shaw saying he thought up his characters and then 'let them rip'. Aristotle is at this point defining the elements of tragedy from the point of view of the audience. What they see happening on the stage is the play.) But merely to define plot as the ordering of incident is hardly sufficient to explain why it should be the very soul of tragedy. Plot is therefore more than a structural stratagem. It is so arranged that it contains within it the essential nature of the play. Because things are rep-resented as happening in this kind of way, the play is this kind of play, just as in a portrait the black and white outline provides the essential representation of the subject (this person and no other person) whereas colour (in drama, characterisation) simply fills in the picture.

The eight and ninth chapters provide authority for what in later ages came to be known as the well-made play. Aristotle's medico-scientific training made him sympathetic to the idea of organic unity. A play should display the signs of its own wholeness. 'Plot' is now used in its simpler structural sense. The action within the play must not be random. Even the story of one man's life fails to measure up to this rigorous structural standard. The argument embraces the virtues of good composition, the placing together of the right elements in the right order, but unfortunately it readily lends itself to giving a special bonus for ingenious but superficial manipulation of the narrative.

Aristotle's reference to universals in his ninth chapter is sufficiently important to merit quotation even in a brief summary:[6]

It is clear from what we have said that it is not the function of the poet to tell what has actually happened but what might or could happen according to probability or necessity. The difference between a historian and a poet does not reside in the use or non-use of metre, for the works of Herodotus could be put in verse, but they would still be history either with or without metre. The difference is that one tells what has happened, the other what might happen. For this reason, poetry is more philosophical and more significant than history for it deals with universals while history deals with particulars.

Neo-classical critics were quick to note the dilemma which this expansion of the concept of mimesis thrust upon them. On the one hand the poet gave an interpretation of the general, not what was but what could be, either in the past or the present or the future. On the other hand he appeared to be obliged to hold a mirror up to Nature and Nature dealt in particulars. How can general truth and particular truth be reconciled? The idea of Horatian decorum indicated a possible compromise. Young men were generally ambitious, hot-tempered, bold; old men were generally irascible, timid, avaricious. Action focussed on the particular could illuminate its general purpose through the utterance of 'sententiae' or aphorisms, a practice taken over very largely from Seneca and often used in seventeenth-century French drama. A further complication arose when Renaissance Platonism was grafted on to the Aristotelian doctrine, as in the case of Sidney, and so the kind of confusion which arises when universals are presumed to equate with an

---

[6] Translated by the authors from the text of the Loeb Classical Library (Heinemann, 1965).

*Introduction: Aristotle and Horace*

ideal morality is exemplified in Samuel Johnson's concern over the portrayal of evil characters in Shakespeare.

Two other topics raised by Aristotle frequently reappear in post-Renaissance essays. They are the anagnorisis or discovery and the definition of the tragic hero. 'An anagnorisis or discovery or recognition, as the name itself makes clear, is a change from ignorance to knowledge, leading either to love or hatred in those marked out for good fortune or disaster.' Neo-classical critics tend to interpret anagnorisis as an item in the mechanics of the plot, an exciting revelation or twist in the story. Some more recent critics see anagnorisis as a central episode in the action leading to the resolution and declaration of the tragic dilemma, wherein the hero enters a state of consciousness which illuminates for him the nature of his existence.[7] Having made his tragic choice, he endures the burning light of tragic awareness, a prelude to his final confrontation with destiny and disaster.

But what kind of person is this hero? Aristotle tells us:[8]

Since the structure of the best tragedy must be not simple but complex and must be a representation of action to excite fear and pity (for this is the essence of such representation) it is initially clear that worthy men must not be shown suffering a change from good to bad fortune. This does not arouse fear or pity but merely disgusts. Nor should wicked men be shown progressing from ill fortune to good. This is the most un-tragic action of all, for it lacks these essentials: it neither appeals to our common humanity nor does it arouse pity or fear. Nor again should a thoroughly bad man be shown falling from good fortune to ill. Such a pattern of events might touch our humanity but would not arouse either pity or fear, since we reserve pity for the man who meets undeserved misfortune and know fear for the man like ourselves but in this case the result

[7] Cf. Maxwell Anderson in *The Essence of Tragedy and other Footnotes and Papers.*     [8] Aristotle. *The Poetics*, ch. 13 (authors' trans.).

11

would produce neither pity nor fear. There remains the midway position. This accounts for the sort of man who is not especially virtuous and just but falls into misfortune not through evil or wickedness but through some flaw in character.

The Greek word *hamartia* here translated 'flaw' has provided critics with a wide area for dispute since it runs through a scale of meaning from simple failure, a mistake through ignorance, a fault or error of judgment, to guilt and sin. One can select one's gravity, as it were, to suit the desired interpretation. A few lines further on, Aristotle says his hero must demonstrate a 'great flaw' but this must not amount to wickedness. Whatever he meant, it is clear he did not expect tragic action to exhibit what later came to be called, in the phrase invented by Thomas Rymer, 'poetic justice'.

After some further comments on fear and pity; on the qualities of characterisation; different kinds of discovery; thought, diction and style, Aristotle concludes his essay with a brief note on the epic and an even briefer comparison between epic and tragedy. The present reader's attention has been particularly directed to those topics detailed above and found in the first thirteen chapters of *The Poetics* because they seem to be significant examples of the kind of Aristotelian comment which attracted post-Renaissance scholars. It is perfectly true, as Elder Olson points out,[9] that 'only the most superficial resemblances can be found between the poetic theory of Aristotle and the theories advanced by neo-classical critics' but he would seem to be driving the argument too hard when he says that 'the general development of neo-classical criticism would have remained much the same had *the Poetics* never figured in it'. Surely the

[9] *Aristotle's Poetics and English Literature,* ed. Olson, Introduction, p. xviii.

fact that the neo-classical critics misunderstood or re-acted against much of *The Poetics* and fabricated an Aristotelian–Horatian hodge-podge was important in providing a point of departure which, if it did not lead them to a 'methodological interpretation' at least encouraged them to investigate and sometimes make thoroughly serviceable statements about the nature of drama.

The reputation and influence of Horace throughout the neo-classical period may well surprise us today since we are in a position to appreciate that the depth and subtlety of Aristotle's comments are of a different order from those of Horace and yet the latter were seized on by neo-classical critics almost as if they had been written before *The Poetics* and were closer to the root of the matter. The reasons for this are several. Doubtless one is that the text of the *Letter to the Pisos*, which, somewhere along the line (certainly by the time Quintilian was writing) had appended to it the misleading subtitle *The Art of Poetry*, had better luck than the text of *The Poetics* in continuing to lead a lively existence throughout the medieval period, being read, referred to and often quoted. Secondly, the early neo-classical critics were still tied to rhetorical modes of analysis and found Horace's dicta suited to their interpretation of the purposes of drama. Thirdly, Horace's aristocratic secure tone attracted those scholars who wished at all costs to found a new culture on the solid rock of the ancients. Horace formed a link with the glories of antiquity, indeed, he was one of them, and at the same time he talked in an accent immediately recognisable by any gentleman of Florence. His emphasis on decorum, propriety, conformism, suited the age.

The letter, and it is no more than an elegantly expressed letter in verse with no pretensions to being a complete treatise on poetry, was addressed to two young men, one of whom apparently had aspirations towards writing. Horace warns the youth of the difficulties facing the poet and in particular the problems of writing for the theatre, which, as he tells us in an earlier Epistle (ii, i) was at this time in a pretty poor state:

Transported to the stage in his air-borne chariot, the poet is dispirited by a slow audience, but an attentive one is an inspiration in itself. By such a slight, such a little circumstance is the peace of a mind anxious for praise made or marred. If I droop when I miss the prize, or grow arrogant when I win, then goodbye to drama. This is the sort of thing that scares off a good poet, the fact that the mob, devoid of rank and decency, ignorant and stupid, ready to start a fight if their betters disagree with them, demand in the middle of the performance a bear or a wrestling match, because that is what the common sort enjoy. In fact, even the upper classes have now transferred their pleasure from their ears to their eyes, from listening to gazing cheerfully at nothing. The curtains are brought down to reveal for four hours or more whole squadrons of horse and platoons of infantry in flight. Kings are dragged on, their hands bound. Chariots, carriages, wagons, ships, move around. Ivory statues are displayed, and the captured spoils of Corinth. If Democritus were here, he would laugh to see how the mob turn their gaze on this *mélange* of camel, leopard and white elephant. He would be more interested in the audience than in the performance and come to the conclusion that the poets were telling their tales to deaf asses. What voice could be heard above the din our theatre makes? You would think you were listening to the moaning of the Apulian grove or the Tuscan sea.[10]

It is not surprising after this that Horace in his letter to the Pisos stresses the importance of good craftsmanship and formal excellence:

A comic subject ought not to be expressed in tragic verse; likewise, the banquet of Thyestes cannot be described in jejune

[10] Horace, *The Epistles*, ed. Wilkins, ii, i, lines 177–202 (authors' trans.).

14

jingles more suited to comedy. Let each separate style maintain its own place once that is allocated to it.[11]

Having considered the kinds of metres suitable to tragedy and comedy, Horace advises the young dramatist to have regard to what nowadays we would call the speaker's register. The character must use the kind of language which fits his station in life. Deeds of violence should not be visibly presented on the stage otherwise there is a danger of the action not being credible. He states that a play should be divided into five acts, apparently on the grounds that Menander adopted this division. Visiting gods and the chorus must know their place and not step out of it. After a long excursus on the history of Greek drama and the unhappy state of the current Roman theatre, he advises the young playwright to model his work on the examples and manners he sees before him:

I will advise the clever playwright to take life and its conduct as his model and so give his dialogue the ring of truth. Oftentimes a credible story with good characterisation even if it lacks elegance, profundity or artistry, gives the people more pleasure and holds their attention better than tinkling trivial verses devoid of matter.[12]

Historically, Horace's most important critical dictum centres on his view that the play must provide instruction as well as pleasure:

Poets want to provide either profit or pleasure, to say things which are at once both pleasant and useful for living...Works created for pleasure should be close to truth. Your play cannot command credence just because it happens to suit you...He

[11] Horace, *De Arte Poetica*, ed. Wilkins, p. 64, lines 89–91 (authors' trans.).
[12] Horace, *De Arte*, lines 317–22.

gains approval who blends instruction with delight, who gives pleasure to his reader along with advice.[13]

This bland urbane prudential essay seems to have been accepted in the sixteenth and seventeenth centuries as virtually a complete theory of poetry. It was neatly squared with Aristotle's *Poetics* and the two works between them provided a body of institutes which could be appealed to for value judgments, revised when necessary and reverenced at all times. Horace is, in the words of Ben Jonson, 'an author of much civility' who seeks to establish a fixed formula for the production of successful literature in the sense of writing which will appeal to readers like himself, 'of much civility'. When an interest in classical criticism was revived in the sixteenth century it was almost inevitable, given the hierarchically structured society of post-Renaissance Europe, that scholars would adopt the formalistic posture of Horace rather than the tentative experimental organic approach of Aristotle. Indeed the latter seems often to be treated as if he had written after Horace and had, as it were, endorsed the Horatian view. Instead of being open and tentative, the new criticism tended for a time to be closed, dogmatic, presented as articles of faith. The techniques of theological debate were forced into a new secular mould in an attempt to provide critical apparatus for literary and dramatic works which often failed to conform to the postulates of the doctrine applied to them.

Although *The Poetics* was known to scholars in Europe and the Middle East from at least the eighth century, translations and commentaries do not take shape until the mid-sixteenth century, by which time many variations of the text are available, including three in Latin

[13] Ibid. lines 33–334, 338, 343.

16

dated 1498, 1515 and 1536. The first scholar to publish a detailed commentary was Francesco Robortello
(1516–1567) whose 'explicationes' appeared in Florence
in 1548.

## 2

# From Robortello to Ben Jonson

Robortello tells us that the end of poetry is to imitate through language and to give delight. Successful imitation has a moral purpose in demonstrating to the audience how others have had to endure suffering. In this witnessing of suffering, the emotions of pity and fear are aroused, along with admiration, a wondering at the marvellous. Although comedy is pleasanter, men write and go to see tragedies because the emotional experience is deeper and writers have the further satisfaction of carrying out a more difficult task. Robortello sets the critical pattern for treating drama primarily as a form of rhetoric, a means of doing something to an audience, of improving them morally. There may be pleasure, but it is secondary to moral improvement.

In 1559 Antonio Minturno published his *De Poeta* wherein as in Robortello the medieval view of tragic action as a story of a man fallen from high degree into misery takes central place. The poet, he says, illustrates how human error brings men of dignity and power into the depths of misfortune. All this is done for our benefit, so that we may learn that no trust can be placed in prosperity and nothing mortal is so durable, so stable, that it may not totter. Thus do we learn to bear our miseries with fortitude and to understand that there is 'nullum malum nisi culpa', no evil but guilt. On catharsis Minturno argues that pity and fear are the best emotions for bringing about a general purgation of all the ills that may attack the human soul, including avarice,

18

pride, the desire to dominate, lechery or any other 'fury of the mind'. When pity and fear are aroused at the prospect of the tragic hero's fate, a spiritual purgation is initiated exactly parallel to the physical purgation induced by an aperient. This process is of course not unaccompanied by pleasure ('Nec sine delectatione perturbat') since the tragic poet excites us by the force of his words and the gravity of his moralising. The individual gains pleasure from poetry, but, and this would seem in the event to be more important for Minturno, he develops an increased regard for virtue through seeing imitations of the fate of others.

Born an Italian, Julius Caesar Scaliger (1484–1558) spent the latter part of his life in the French town of Agen where he started a medical school and is reputed to have had Rabelais as a student until they quarrelled. When Erasmus published an attack on Cicero in 1528, Scaliger joined in the controversy in favour of Cicero. He evolved a system of Latin grammar for his son Silvius, to whom he also addressed his defence of poetry entitled *Seven Essays on Poetry* (*Poetices Libri Septem*) which was published three years after his death and became one of the standard reference books of the neo-classical critics. Scaliger's interpretation of Aristotle, with its strong injection of Horatian ideas on decorum and its alignment with medieval morality, reflected the prevalent thinking of his times and appealed to readers who for at least a generation afterwards shared his assumptions and accepted his postulates without question.

Tragedy differs from comedy, says Scaliger, in three ways:[1] in the status of the characters; in the nature of their fortunes and affairs; and in the ending. It follows there will be a difference in style. In comedy a Chremes, a Davus, a Thais, are

---

[1] Quotations are translated from the fifth edition of *Poetices Libri Septem* (1617).

people of humble estate. There is confusion at the beginning and happiness at the end...In tragedy there are kings and princes from cities and citadels and from around camps. The beginnings are full of foreboding and the endings terrible.

Here with possibly some little debt to Donatus, Scaliger defines the proper matter of tragedy, expanding Aristotle's 'highly renowned and prosperous' in terms of courtly splendour and chivalry. Likewise, he continues:

The dialogue is grave and refined, far removed from the vulgar tongue; the whole atmosphere is one of uncertainty, fear, threats, exile and death. The story goes that Euripides was asked by Archelaus, king of Macedonia, in whose care and patronage he lived, to write a tragedy about him. 'No, in heaven's name', he said, 'ask not for so much misery'. (Book I, ch. VI)

Thus the presence of the tragic hero is signalled by rank and an unhappy ending. Kings and princes have by their position a tragic potential lacking in the humbler estates. In conformity with Horace's doctrine concerning decorum, there should be a special language for tragedy, grave and refined.

Scaliger now goes on to quote Aristotle's definition of tragedy in the original Greek and comments:

I have no objection to this and merely wish to add something of my own...[Tragedy] is a representation, by means of incidents, of a noble fate. It has an unhappy ending and it is written in serious verse. Though the verses add harmony and song, the verse itself is not, in the words of the philosophers, of the essence of tragedy. Tragedy if this were so would exist only on the stage; never off the stage. As to his statement, that it had certain limitations in its length, he means that it differs from epic poetry, which is sometimes prolix, although not always. You see an example of this in Musaeus. The term 'catharsis' fits neither sort of medium. Megathos here means 'measure' or

20

'moderation'. The anticipation of the crowd is not satisfied by only a few words for they are making up for many dreary days by looking forward to a few hours of pleasure. Equally, excessive length is unsuitable...as Plautus says, 'Their limbs become painful through sitting and their eyes through watching'. (ch. VI)

Scaliger is here breaking away from Aristotle and adopting the Horatian-Ciceronian-Medieval view of poetry as being a form of rhetoric, a means of pleasurable instruction rather than a human activity (imitation) to which man is naturally attracted and which provides its own justification. Tragedy, says Scaliger, is concerned with kings and princes who suffer an unhappy fate which is described in appropriately elevated diction. On catharsis he has practically nothing to say. Aristotle's view that a play has organically its own proper length because it is that kind of artefact and not something else is interpreted in coarser terms related directly to audience response. Since the audience is there to be instructed it must not have avoidable discomfort inflicted upon it. The more comfortable it is, the more accessible it will be to the moral lesson.

Towards the end of Book I, Scaliger raises some technical points regarding the definition of a scene.

A scene is part of the act in which two or more characters speak; it begins sometimes by the entrance of all the characters, sometimes only of one, who then finds someone else remaining from the previous scene; it is finished sometimes by the exit of everyone, sometimes by the exit of only one character. So if there were three, the two who remained would come into the following scene...The chorus is the part between the acts. But we also see the chorus at the end of plays. So a safer definition would be to say that the chorus is that part which comes after the act and is accompanied by music. (Book I, ch. IX)

Scaliger is here searching for a logic of structure and in so doing established a rule for the linking of scenes which became standard practice in the French seventeenth-century theatre. He makes no attempt to examine the part played by the chorus in developing and commenting on the action and directing the attention of the audience.

In Book VII, ch. II (p. 830) he turns again to Aristotle's theory of mimesis and rejects it as inadequate:

Aristotle makes the poet's whole purpose to be concerned with imitation which he attributes as peculiar to man among all living things. Although indeed he continually cherished this stated opinion and often repeated it, he leads us into two absurdities. One is when he links together not only poetry as a class in itself but epic as a sub-division of it along with the mimes of Sophron and the prose dialogues of Alexamen of Teos on philosophy. The other is when he says that the history of Herodotus, if it had been written in metre, would nonetheless be history. The first is absurd because he makes epic poetry a kind of prose. Contrariwise, with history this will not be so, for it will not be history but historical poetry. All this is on account of the fact that the end of poetry is not imitation but pleasurable teaching whereby the minds of men may be led into right reason. In this wise, man achieves perfect action, which we call Happiness (*Beatitudo*). But if nothing but imitation were the end of poetry, anyone who imitated would be a poet. So the character of Socrates in the *Dialogues* and the orator playing his part are (in this sense) poets. Even Plato will be a poet in his *Laws*, those *Laws* from which he excluded the poet.

Philip Sidney, whether or not he had this passage in mind, used a similar argument to demonstrate that in fact Plato *was* a poet when he had recourse to imagery. The gist of the argument thus far is fairly clear. Imitation in itself is almost a frivolous occupation. Poetry has a stouter task in front of it.

So, in discussing the relationship between character

22

and action in Book VII, ch. III Scaliger starts from the position that philosophers postulate a model or ideal of worthy actions which they call right reason (*ratio recta*). While vicious actions do not provide any kind of corresponding model (i.e. there cannot be wrong reason) we must accept that without evil there could be neither goodness nor badness:[2]

What therefore does the poet teach? That actions proceed from a state of mind which we call a disposition? Or does he show the path by which we may avoid such actions; [does he show] the source of good conduct and the right way to shun evil crimes?

This view that the poet has a responsibility for the moral education of his audience prepares us for what follows and provides an advance warning of the kind of misinterpretation to which Aristotle is to be subjected:

Aristotle had this to say: Since poetry is to be compared to that institution of state which leads us to happiness (*ad beatitudinem*) and happiness is in effect nothing more than perfect action, a poem will not in any way lead to the development of character but to the development of action. Rightly so, and in truth we would not believe otherwise. But he adds something a little more difficult, for he says you cannot have tragedy without action but you can have tragedy without disposition – for I am inclined in this context thus to translate *ethos* which is [normally] character-in-itself. For he says tragic poets of his own time generally wrote plays 'without character'. Thus Zeuxis did not express character in his works but Polygnotus was a fine delineator of character. If then character (*ethos*) is [interpreted as] a disposition towards [a certain kind of] action and it is excluded from tragic action, everything will happen by chance or contingency. For instance, in one play, Orestes killed

[2] *Translators' note:* In order to make the following passage read with any kind of connected sense, it has been found necessary to expand certain words and phrases. The interpolations are within square brackets.

his mother but this was not 'character in action' (*ethos*) for he did not perform the deed in accordance with his character. But Aegisthus acted in character and so did Polymnester, Pylades, Euclio, Pseudolus, Ballio and Davus. So we do not ask whether the poet teaches character or action but whether he teaches [us] about disposition or consequences. For although many things are done out of character, nothing is done without there being a tendency (*affectus*) to do it. This is the question then but the answer is to be found in what has been said before. The poet teaches us about tendencies [to act in a certain way] through [describing] action so that we may admire good men and imitate their actions; so that we may scorn bad men and refrain from crimes. [Presentation of] action is therefore the method of teaching; and tendencies [implicated towards certain kinds of action] are the material which we are taught so that we too may act [rightly]. Therefore [presentation of] action will be as it were an example or instrument in the plot and [revelation of] tendencies will be the real purpose. But in the state, action is the end and tendencies [towards action] will become the model. (p. 832)

At this point it is surely appropriate to quote Scaliger's next remark: 'If this appears to anyone to be more subtle than the question demands, let him not be annoyed at our zeal'. However, the apparent complexity of the argument may be simplified if we understand that Scaliger here proposes a theory of psychology which by means of a semantic subterfuge leads him to an ethical theory appropriate to the function of the poet and the nature of the state as he saw them. His psychological theory (it may or may not be relevant to recall that as well as being secretary to a bishop, Scaliger set up a medical school) postulates two aspects to man's character, one being fixed, determined and final (*mores*) the other mutable, possibly improvable and showing itself by a tendency to do certain things in certain situations (*affectus*) so that a man (like Orestes) may be in character while acting out of character (*mores*). To derive the meaning he wants from Aristotle's 'tragedy is possible without character but not without action', he gives Aristotle's word 'ethos' a double burden to bear. (Again we might recall he wrote a book on grammar which became a standard work used long after his death.) The referents to *ethos* may be either *mores*, fixed character, or *affectus*, a disposition or tendency to do certain things.

He agrees thus far with Aristotle that the poem, or play, is not concerned with delineating fixed character but with describing action (*neutiqua ad mores consequendos deducet poema, sed ad facta ipsa*). But, his argument proceeds, if Aristotle is trying to tell us that you can have tragedy without the persons in it showing some tendency to act in a certain way, this will not do, for the action, with its tragic denouement, would be contingent, accidental. Orestes' killing of his mother would thus be a mere accident since he was not the sort of person who would normally kill his mother. But apart from his normal character (*mores*) there is that within him (*affectus*) which makes it possible for him to commit matricide. So although the plot may exist *praeter mores* it cannot exist *sine affectu*. Serious poets therefore tell us about people's tendencies or dispositions through their actions. The action is the medium, the disposition is the message. This is done so that we may become acquainted with right and wrong dispositions and make a wise choice among those dispositions we favour. We will thus model ourselves on those persons in the play who demonstrate sound dispositions and so, in turn, our own conditioned tendencies, as we might say today, will result in right action within the state. Tragedy, through its presentation of action, illuminates worthy characteristics in its persons and this illumination is the beginning and the end of the poet's function (*affectus verso finis*). As public servants however, our dispositions (strengthened and guided by the models we have seen) will reveal themselves in our actions and it is sound action within the state which is the real end of living (*actio erit finis*).

Scaliger envisages poetry as being one element in a complex of social activities which involves ethics and politics and is concerned with assisting the community towards some sort of harmony or happiness (*beatitudo*) through proper action but such action will be the consequence of sound character formation which will be helped by seeing good models. So poets must strive to offer exemplary characters, and action is needed in the play mainly to provide a field for the display of virtue or the punishment of vice. The audience must understand that certain people have certain tendencies to action, either good or bad, and appropriate action will demonstrate that good tendencies lead to a good end and bad to bad. Outside the world of fiction, in the real world of things, action leading to the general weal of the state is what is required but this can only come as a consequence of the people possessing that kind of moral excellence which the example of imaginary characters created by the poets may help them to achieve. In an age when the authority of the church is waning, the people more than ever need good examples set before them. If the fear of hell is less effective than it used to be, the threat of earthly miseries awaiting the sinner may encourage a willing acceptance of the prevalent social code and that after all is what these aristocratic philosopher-critics held to be the first function of poetry.

Although it would be an exaggeration to say that these three commentaries owe more to Horace, Cicero and Quintilian than they do to Aristotle, the fact remains that the spirit in which they are written is closer to the Roman writers than to the Greek. To teach, to delight, to move, the triple function of Ciceronian rhetoric, lies behind the argument. Teaching means encouraging the highest standards of behaviour in citizens and nobility of thought and action in private individuals. It is assumed, of course, that only a limited section of the population is capable of such nobility, but their example will be of value to the weaker members. The poet's imitations are good in so far as they persuade the audience that these things could have happened and the characters at the centre of the action behave with enough credibility to make their responses to the dramatic situation telling, vivid, provocative of admiration and therefore exemplary. Pleasure is an attendant emotion and its precise placing in the dramatic scale of values is open to question but even in Minturno one gets the final impression that learning comes above enjoyment in value even though they are simultaneous experiences. The contrast offered by the fourth member of the group, Castelvetro, is that while he chose to controvert practically everything he understood Aristotle to mean, he approaches the play in a genuinely Aristotelian spirit, as an artefact, made up by a poet in accordance with certain limiting conditions for the purpose of giving pleasure to a certain kind of audience.

Ludovico Castelvetro (1505–1571) was the son of a wealthy bourgeois family of Modena. He published his translation of and commentary on Aristotle's *Poetics* in 1570 while enjoying the protection of the Emperor Maximilian. Like Scaliger but with less good fortune he was accused of heresy and remained outside Italy for the last ten years of his life. He writes in the high-minded tone of an intellectual who suspects that drama is more suited to the entertainment of the mob than to the exposition of moral and spiritual insights or patterns of good behaviour. Poetry operates on a different level from the sciences and the arts;[3]

---

[3] Quotations are translated from the second edition of *La Poetica d'Aristotele Vulgarizzata et Sposta* (1576).

Furthermore, for another reason more immediately apprehended, the content (*materia*) of the sciences and the arts cannot be the subject of poetry because poetry was invented solely for delight and recreation, for the purpose, I assure you, of delighting and amusing the minds of the rude multitude and the common people. Such people understand neither reasons nor categories nor subtle arguments beyond the pale of halfwits, arguments such as used by philosophers in investigating the truth about things or by artists in the ordonnance of their art. When others speak in an incomprehensible manner beyond the usual run of things, they, in their lack of suitable comprehension, are bored and displeased. (p. 29)

For the first time we find a rejection of the Ciceronian 'docere' and the Horatian 'dulce et utile'. As far as Castelvetro is concerned, poetry, including drama, is a source of popular entertainment. The common people are stupid; they cannot comprehend philosophy; they are capable only of listening to amusing fiction. Neither science nor philosophy, he argues, can find their way into poetry because this would be to intellectualise a mode of statement intended for the unintellectual. This argument involves a transposition of emphasis which would have puzzled Aristotle even although he might have recognized its derivation in his own view that poetry was concerned with giving a certain kind of pleasure through offering a certain kind of imitation of the real world. For Aristotle, poetry created its own world. For Castelvetro, poetry offers a substitute world which must never move too far away from the world as perceived, experienced, heard, felt, tasted by the rude multitude.

The unsuitability of science and philosophy to poetry is complemented by an ambiguous treatment of moral questions. The tragic hero is not identified by his goodness or wickedness but solely on the strength of his nobility which is a function of his courtliness, natural wit, cleverness.

28

So it appears that nobility or baseness constitutes the difference in poetry as far as subject matter is concerned. Such nobility or baseness does not show itself in goodness or wickedness but in deportment. A decorous bearing reveals nobility whereas baseness is declared by lack of good breeding. And by decorum and its opposite I mean manners and civility which do not bear witness to the goodness or wickedness of a person's mind, but testify to the courtliness or rusticity of a man and are derived from his natural wit, that is to say, from his cleverness or stupidity. (p. 36)

So much has been written about the unities and so many misconceptions disseminated that the discovery of the actual source comes almost like a moment of revelation. They have even been called the 'Aristotelian unities' though Aristotle mentions but one, the unity of action. They have been fathered on to Scaliger who merely mentions time and place in passing. Here in *La Poetica d'Aristotele* is the original formulation: first the unity of time:

The limited time in which the audience can remain seated in the theatre cannot as I see it exceed one revolution of the sun, as Aristotle says, that is, twelve hours, because, on account of their bodily needs, such as eating, drinking, getting rid of the superfluities in belly and bladder, sleeping and so on, the people cannot remain in the theatre beyond the aforementioned time. (p. 109)

Unity of place follows from unity of time. Since the audience are so lacking in imagination, they cannot be expected to believe in anything that is not set in front of them. Oddly enough, Castelvetro did not put this restriction on epic where 'intellectual time' is allowed to operate (i.e. imaginative time). In the theatre however, what is not seen cannot be believed and since it is the object of the playwright to give pleasure through achieving verisimilitude, he must not put undue pressure on his audience's credibility. Unity of action, the one unity which Aristotle clearly prizes, is not insisted on but is recommended for reasons which have nothing to do with the organic structure of the play but follow again from the limitation of the audience's intelligence:

But Aristotle has strongly advised that in tragedy and comedy the plot should maintain only a single action (or two so interdependent as to be considered one) and should be about one person rather than a whole race of people.

This is not because the plot is incapable of sustaining more action but because the length of time of not more than twelve hours in which the action is to be represented does not allow of a multitude of actions nor even the action of one family nor, often enough, even one complete and entire action if it is of some length. This is the principal and necessary reason why the plot of a tragedy or a comedy must be one, that is to say, must contain one action only concerning one person or two actions considered as one because they are closely interdependent. (p. 179)

Given that it is the first duty of the poet to amuse and hold the attention of an ignorant audience, Castelvetro lays down 'verisimilitude' as the essential dramatic quality. By verisimilitude he appears to mean a homogeneous relationship as complete as possible, between the poetic statement and reality. The word must as nearly as possible equal the thing. What we nowadays call 'fictional documentary' would have his approval – an imagined tale supported by so much naturalistic and credible data that it looks like a true story. This is not to say that he confuses life and art. Actions should be *possibili avenire, ma non gia avenute*, capable of having happened but without actually having happened. What then is the difference between poetry and history? In sum, very little and it is even possible to conceive of poetry as a branch of history, a kind of entertaining pseudo-history. Tragedy, dealing as it does with kings and princes, must be based on historical events but should not *be* history. The difference is that history happened, tragedy did not. History deals in truth (*verita*) tragedy seeks for verisimilitude (*verisimilitudine*). The poet walks the tightrope between truth and fiction, leaning as near to truth as possible without ever narrating true things, i.e. things which actually happened. This grafting of fiction on to truth or truth on to fiction – for so fine is the balance that the parent could be either truth or fiction – is a difficult task for the tragic poet, and success, while giving his audience pleasure, brings him the greater glory. The final arbiter in every case is the audience. Has it believed the story and has it been suitably entertained not by a bald narration of facts but by a vividly told story spiced with 'the marvellous'?

Although Castelvetro argues that the purpose of drama is to amuse an audience, he cannot complete his commentary without reference to the moral content at least of tragedy, if not comedy. His division between the two is based on the public status of his characters.

Those characters in tragedy are regal and have greater spirits and are more noble; their aspirations are unbounded and if they are insulted or an injury is intended against them, they do not have recourse to the magistrates to take legal action against the offender nor do they bear the injury patiently but they make their own judgements and kill in vendettas both distant and close relatives and not only blood relations but sometimes, in despair, even themselves...

But the characters of comedy, men of little courage, are accustomed to obey the magistrates and to live under the law, to put up with insult and injury and to make their supplications to officials who give them restitution and amends for their injuries through the law.   (p. 222)

While the above, despite its Horatian ancestry, may throw more light on the aristocratic social attitudes of

31

Renaissance humanism than on the nature of tragedy and comedy, Castelvetro later enters into more serious debate with Aristotle on moral issues. He assumes that Aristotle agrees with him that poetry in general is invented for the purpose of giving pleasure but is concerned to notice that, according to his reading, Aristotle looks in tragedy mainly for utility.

If poetry is invented principally for delight and not for utility, as Aristotle has demonstrated when he speaks of the origin of poetry in general, why does he wish that in tragedy, which is one kind of poetry, we look mainly for utility? Why do we not look for delight without caring about utility? (p. 275)

He continues the argument by denying the premise which he claims Aristotle has laid down and then seeks for an explanation of the apparently contradictory idea that a sad story can give pleasure. Clearly, our pleasure must derive from a sense of recognition of the injustice of the hero's fate. He takes his stand on the difference between the moral utility of purgation and the emotional pleasure of sympathising sadly with a man deserted by fortune. This gives a *diletto obliquo*, an oblique pleasure, as distinct from the *diletto diritto* or straightforward pleasure we experience in seeing a good man pass from misery to happiness which is the proper matter of comedy. Both emotions are pleasurable and both can stand in their own right, without the support of any theory of purgation to justify the poet's 'utility'. The argument, it will be noticed, looks curiously ahead to eighteenth-century concepts of sentimentalism.

Castelvetro is not an easy critic to summarise. He is an original. 'Inventor' of the rule of unities, he feels himself bound by no rules. His approach is pragmatic. He does not, like Aristotle, ask: what does a tragedy consist of? He prefers the question: what does a tragedy do? In that sense but in that sense alone, he is a Ciceronian, treating drama as a branch of rhetoric. His answer to the question denies the Ciceronian 'docere'. A tragedy, he claims persistently, exists to give pleasure to a certain kind of audience and from that point onwards his argument is consistent.

Is he so far wrong when he says that plays are written to please audiences; that audiences in the main fail to respond to too much intellectualising; that plays have to be presented in a limited time (unlike epic poetry or the novel) and therefore make a concentrated attack on a narrow front, in time, in location and in structure; that audiences like plays to bear a pretty close resemblance to what they consider 'real life' to be about; that at the same time they dislike too much actuality ('history') and accept a reasonable dosage of the 'marvellous'; that they like to see a good man rewarded at the end and if he comes to grief they weep for him pleasurably, sentimentally? Castelvetro said all these things. If accepted as an interpretation of Aristotle, they would be perverse to the point of being outrageous, but then they are not so intended. They are the independent conclusions of a man who apparently set no great store by the intellectual content, spiritual insights or moral enlightenment of tragedy as it affected the kind of audience he had in mind, but who endeavoured, while aware of the position he had taken up, to argue inductively from the examples of drama which he knew. He is careful in his definition of verisimilitude not to confuse life and art. Art is an imitation of life so organised as to give pleasure but still bound by the laws of nature of which it is itself a part. The poet works within these limitations and in overcoming them brings glory on himself while at the same time not losing sight of his duty to his audience.

It will be apparent so far that the humanist rediscovery

of *The Poetics* was encouraging European scholars to formulate a body of rules for the composition and criticism of poetry in its widest sense. While Minturno and Scaliger state clearly that poetry should be doctrinal and Castelvetro is equally clear that its purpose is to give pleasure, they all endeavour in their different ways and within their limitations to treat literature on its own terms as a made thing, composed by men out of words and subject to certain rules which have their origin in the nature of the material, the quality of mind and intention of the maker, and the characteristics, the assumed response, of the reader or audience. Thus far, they are literary critics in any sense of the phrase, concerned about words, about structure, about the author's insights, about the power of the literary artefact to persuade or to please.

This kind of writing, professional in tone and devoted to the technicalities of its subject, takes longer to appear in England, and the first sustained essay on criticism, summarising the works of the Italian scholars and adding its own special and on occasion remarkable insights is Sir Philip Sidney's *An Apologie for Poetry* written about 1581 and not published until 1595. The two titles of the work, *Apology*, and in another version *Defence*, point to the motivation behind the work. Serious writing in England at this time is dominated by the two themes of politics and ethics. Books abound on the model of Machiavelli's *Prince*, advice to rulers on how to rule, and plays are expected to carry on the morality tradition of demonstrating man's endless struggle throughout his life to avoid evil and seek the good. The history of English theatrical performances in the sixteenth century is a tale of changing fashions, changing laws and changing demands. As the century moves into its second half, miracle plays are frowned on as relics of the old papist days (as are the Robin Hood plays previously acted throughout the country even as far north as Aberdeen) and even moralities, encouraged in the beginning by the reformers, come to be suspected by Protestant church- men along with all other 'vaine playes or enterludes'. John Stockwood, schoolmaster of Tunbridge, preaches at St Paul's Cross on St Bartholomew's Day, 1578:[4]

Will not a fylthye playe, wyth the blast of a Trompette, sooner call thyther a thousand, than an hours tolling of a Bell bring to the Sermon a hundred? nay even heere in the Citie, without it be at this place, and some other certaine ordinarie audience, where shall you finde a reasonable company? whereas, if you resort to the Theatre, the Curtayne, and other places of Playes in the Citie, you shall on the Lords day have these places, with many others that I can not reckon, so full, as possible they can throng, besides a great number of other lettes, to pull from the hearing of the word, of which I will speake heereafter.

A piece of writing more closely associated with Sidney's *Apologie* is Stephen Gosson's *The School of Abuse contain- ing a pleasant invective against Poets, Pipers, Plaiers, Iestors and such like Caterpillars of a Commonwealth* published in 1579 with a dedication to Sidney which, on the authority of correspondence between Spencer and Gabriel Harvey Sidney 'scorned'. Gosson, a scholar of Christ Church, came down in 1576 at the age of twenty-one and set about writing plays and poems and even, it appears, acting on the stage. Three years later he turns against the craft and writes *The School of Abuse*. He died in 1624, the respected rector of St Botolph, Bishopsgate. *The School of Abuse* is a wide-ranging piece of invective against all those social activities which Gosson from the wisdom of twenty-four years, claimed to dislike on account of their depravity. No case is made: he denounces, airs his classical learning and leaves the matter. It does Sidney a disservice to call his carefully reasoned document a specific answer to

[4] Quoted from Arber's Introduction, to S. Gosson, *The School of Abuse*.

Gosson's verbose tirade although he may have Gosson's unreadable prose style in mind when he denounces those scholars and preachers whose eloquence is apparelled in 'a Curtizan-like painted affectation'.

*The School of Abuse* while worthless as criticism, directs us to an understanding of the critical position Sidney found it necessary to take up when he set about his *Apologie*. Poetry, including the poetry of the stage, had to be defended against the abuse of clever young men who doubtless felt that preferment might lie with a thorough-going conservatism in cultural matters. Sidney was fortunate in his family background and with his unequivocal status as an aristocrat, he brought moral courage, a well stocked mind and a keen wit to 'the defence of that my unelected vocation' of Poet.

He starts boldly by claiming that all knowledge owes its origins to the writings of poets, with a shrewd thrust at Plato who was something of a poet when he created his dialogues, a dramatic fiction. Plato is again under attack when Sidney claims that the poet, far from offering the shadow of a shadow, creates a new kind of nature, a golden world far surpassing the brazen world that we know from Nature. Poetry is 'an Art of Imitation: for so Aristotle termeth it in the word Mimesis, that is to say, a representing counterfeiting or figuring forth to speak metaphorically. A speaking Picture, with this end to teach and to delight.' After the bold suggestion that the poets create an ideal world, Sidney returns us to familiar Scaligerian territory. But, he goes on, there are three kinds of imitators: the prophets of religion; the philosophers (moral, natural, historical, astronomical) and the true poets who in their imitating, borrow 'nothing of what is, hath been or shall be'. Both the historian and the moral philosopher challenge the poet but retire before his greater ability to teach and simultaneously to give pleasure. The historian's teaching is limited by his bondage to the factual, the particular; the moral philosopher teaches, but his 'sullen gravity' gives no pleasure. The poet provides both precept and example and presents them in a pleasurable form. Even Christ was a poet when he taught through the pleasing fiction of the parable.

We are now firmly placed in the neo-classic ground of teaching – moving – pleasing. The 'high and excellent' tragedy ensures that evil men are punished and good rewarded (history often shows the reverse). The great wounds and ulcers of life are shown forth in tragedy. Comedy is an imitation of the common errors of life represented in the most ridiculous and scornful sort. Critics of poetry are smartly dealt with. It is neither time-wasting nor profitless. It tells no lies because the poet 'nothing affirms and therefore never lyeth'. It commits no abuse except when it is itself abused, as a sword destined for the defence of one's country may be used to kill a father and even if Plato banished poets it should be remembered that a philosopher is the natural enemy of poets and furthermore Plato himself is not innocent of loose talk (the *Symposium*) or of encouraging community of women as in his *Republic*.

Anxious as he is to justify the ways of poetry to men, when he considers native drama Sidney finds himself reduced to turning over barren soil. We must remember that he wrote before the appearance of Lily, Kyd or Marlowe, not to mention Shakespeare and Jonson. He had no sympathy for the popular theatre which went on its way regardless of 'rules', owing more in its structural devices to the medieval cycles of miracle plays than to the central idea of formal unity. Even *Gorboduc*, a contrived literary play close to the classical model, was insufficiently rigorous for his taste.[5]

[5] Quotations are from the Ponsonby quarto as reprinted in the Feuillerat edition of Sidney's works, vol. III.

Our Tragidies and Commedies, not without cause cryed out against, observing rules neither of honest civilitie, nor skilfull Poetrie. Excepting Gorboducke, (againe I say of those that I have seen) which notwithstanding as it is full of stately speeches, and well sounding phrases, clyming to the height of Seneca his style, and as full of notable morallitie, which it dooth most delightfully teach, and so obtaine the very ende of Poesie. Yet in truth, it is verie defectious in the circumstances, which greeves mee, because it might not remaine as an exact modell of all Tragidies. For it is faultie both in place and time, the two necessarie Companions of all corporall actions. For where the Stage should alway represent but one place, and the uttermoste time presupposed in it, should bee both by Aristotles precept, and common reason, but one day; there is both manie dayes and places, inartificially imagined. But if it bee so in Gorboducke, howe much more in all the rest, where you shall have Asia on the one side, and Affricke of the other, and so manie other under Kingdomes, that the Player when he comes in, must ever begin with telling where he is, or else the tale will not be conceived. Now you shall have three Ladies walke to gather flowers, and then we must beleeve the stage to be a garden. By and by we heare newes of shipwrack in the same place, then we are too blame if we accept it not for a Rock. Upon the back of that, comes out a hidious monster with fire and smoke, and then the miserable beholders are bound to take it for a Cave: while in the meane time two Armies flie in, represented with foure swords & bucklers, and the what hard hart will not receive it for a pitched field. Now of time, they are much more liberall. For ordinarie it is, that two yoong Princes fall in love, after many traverses she is got with childe, delivered of a faire boy: he is lost, groweth a man, falleth in love, and is readie to get an other childe, and all this in two houres space: which howe absurd it is in sence, even sence may imagine: and Arte hath taught, and all aunciente examples justified, and at this day the ordinarie players in Italie will not erre in. Yet will some bring in an example of Eunuche in Terence, that conteineth matter of two dayes, yet far short of twentie years. True it is, and so was it to be played in two dayes, and so fitted to the time it set foorth. And though Plautus have

38

on one place done amisse, let us hit it with him, & not misse with him. But they will say, how then shall we set foorth a storie, which contains both many places, and many times? And do they not know that a Tragidie is tied to the lawes of Poesie and not of Historie: not bounde to follow the storie, but having libertie either to faine a quite new matter, or to frame the Historie to the most Tragicall conveniencie. Againe, many things may be told which cannot be shewed: if they know the difference betwixt reporting and representing. As for example, I may speake though I am here, of Peru, and in speech digresse from that, to the description of Calecut: But in action, I cannot represent it without Pacelots Horse. And so was the manner the Auncients tooke, by some Nuntius, to recount things done in former time or other place. Lastly, if they will represent an Historie, they must not (as Horace saith) beginne ab ovo, but they must come to the principall poynte of that one action which they will represent. (pp. 38–9)

Here surely is an echo of Sidney's reading of Castelvetro. The power to establish a world complete in itself and subject to its own laws is one of the poet's privileges but even in the act of creating his noble fictions, he is limited by the demands of verisimilitude. Why should we not believe the stage to be a garden when we see three ladies walking to gather flowers? In shying away from the full import of Castelvetro's argument that the only reason is the ignorance, the lack of imagination, of the rude multitude, the audience, Sidney is driven to take refuge in the classical prescription and to conclude that wide tracts of time and place may be spanned by a messenger or chorus, as long as the visual unity of the piece, what is shown on the stage, remains intact.

The possibility of a new drama growing from native roots alien to the classical tradition never struck Sidney or his contemporaries. Conscious as he undoubtedly was of the need for a national identity and national glory in literature, Sidney found little evidence of special distinction in the theatre around him. He was, we may say suavely, looking for the wrong things, but he was using the only guides available to him. It is therefore not surprising that he expressed disgust at 'mungrell Tragycomedie':

But besides these gross absurdities, howe all their Playes bee neither right Tragedies, nor right Comedies, mingling Kinges and Clownes, not because the matter so carrieth it, but thrust in the Clowne by head and shoulders to play a part in majesticall matters, with neither decencie nor discretion: so as neither the admiration and Commiseration, nor the right sportfulnesse is by their mongrell Tragicomedie obtained. I know Apuleius did somewhat so, but that is a thing recounted with space of time, not represented in one moment: and I know the Auncients have one or two examples of Tragicomedies, as Plautus hath Amphitrio. But if we marke them well, wee shall finde that they never or verie daintily matche horne Pipes and Funeralls.   (pp. 39–40)

He closes his remarks on the contemporary theatre with a trenchant comment on the sources of different kinds of humour.

So falleth it out, that having indeed no right Comedy, in that comicall part of our Tragedy, we have nothing but scurrility, unwoorthy of any chast eares: or some extreame shew of doltishness, indeed fit to lift up a loude laughter, and nothing els: where the whole tract of a Comedy, shoulde be full of delight, as the Tragedy shoulde be still maintained, in a well raised admiration. But our Comedians, thinke there is no delight without laughter, which is very wrong, for though laughter may come with delight, yet cometh it not of delight: as though delight should be the cause of laughter, but well may one thing breed both together: nay, rather in themselves, they have as it were, a kind of contrarietie; for delight we scarcely doe, but in things that have a conveniencie to our selves, or to the general nature, laughter, almost ever cometh, of things most disproportioned to ourselves, and nature. Delight hath a joy in it, either permanent, or present. Laughter, hath onely a scornful tickling.   (p. 40)

He draws a distinction between comedy and farce, objecting to the preponderance of farce and the absence of comedy based on thoughtful laughter in the theatre of his day. *Gammer Gurton's Needle* is an example of the good old rustic joke which merits a belly laugh without either the sympathetic undertones of true comedy which his poetic insight encouraged him to demand or the serious criticism of morals which his classical and neo-classical mentors stipulated as the foundation of comedy. One can feel sure that he would have accepted the comedies of Shakespeare and Jonson as being concerned with things not disproportioned to ourselves but rather having a 'convenience' or applicability to our human state.

Looking at the *Defence* in its historical context and having regard to its literary sources, we can appreciate both its adherence to the tradition and its novel insights. The latter have achieved their fair share of repute largely as a consequence of Sidney's vivid expression: the contrast of the 'golden' world with the 'brazen'; the aphoristic pungency of 'he nothing affirmes, and therefore never lyeth'; the picture of the historian with his 'mouse-eaten records' and the philosophers approaching 'with a sullen gravity'. The essay as a whole is however written strictly in the neo-classic continental tradition. Scaliger is mentioned by name but Castelvetro is never far away and at times, as we might expect, they make uneasy bedfellows. Sidney accepts without question the prevalent view (questioned only by Castelvetro) that the first purpose of poetry as of all 'earthly learning' is to lead to virtuous action. The golden world may be of the poet's own creation as, lifted up by the vigour of his invention he

41

ranges outwith the narrow warrant of Nature's gifts, but he creates not in order to bring glory to himself and pleasure to his audience, nor driven by a disinterested urge to make imitations which will establish their own special kind of reality; he creates his world so that it may be exemplary, doctrinal, 'offering whatsoever is most worthy to be learned'. In the end it is the voice of the doctor from Agen which can be heard behind the accents of the English knight, although Sidney puts up a bolder defence for poetry in declaring that not only is poetry significant as a form of human learning, it is the supreme form of human learning. 'Nature never set foorth the earth in so rich Tapistry as divers Poets have done.'

While working on his plays, Ben Jonson (1573–1637) gives a running commentary on how, in his view, plays should be written, and since his starting point as a theorist was clearly Sidney's *Defence*, he is an important link in the chain of discourse stretching from the Italian critics to Dryden. The *Prologue to Every Man In His Humour* did not appear in print until the publication of the 1616 folio of Jonson's works, supervised by himself, but the references, including a side-kick at Shakespeare's historical epics, seem to place it in 1598, the year of the original Italianate version of the play and three years after the publication of the two Sidney editions:[6]

To make a child, new swadled, to proceede
Man, and then shoote up, in one beard and weede,
Past threescore yeeres: or with three rustie swords,
And help of some few foot-and-halfe-foote words,
Fight over *Yorke*, and *Lancasters* long iarres;
He rather prayes, you will be pleas'd to see
One such, to day as other playes should be.
Where neither *Chorus* wafts you ore the seas;

[6] Quoted from *The Works of Ben Jonson*, eds. C. H. Herford, P. & E. Simpson.

Nor creaking throne comes downe, the boyes to please;
Nor nimble squibbe is seene, to make afear'd
The gentlewomen; nor roul'd bullet heard
To say, it thunders; nor tempestuous drumme
Rumbles, to tell you when the storm doth come;

But deedes, and language, such as men doe use;
And persons, such as Comoedie would chuse,
When she would shew an Image of the times
And sport with humane follies, not with crimes.
Except, we make 'hem such by loving still
Our popular errors, when we know th'are ill.
I mean such errors, as you'll all confesse
By laughing at them, they deserve no lesse:
Which when you heartily doe, there's hope left, then,
You, that have so grac'd monsters, may like men.   (folio 1616)
(vol. III, p. 303)

In its dogmatic tone, this amalgam of Sidney and Horace
takes us back to the puritan polemic of Gosson and his
contemporaries. The young writer is determined to be
out of step with his rivals by declaring himself an
ultra-conservative, a student of the neo-classical rule
book. Spectacle, stage effects, the coarse thrill that
originates in the carpenter's shop and the tiring house
rather than in the study, are to retire before the superior
figure of true Comedy, defined in Ciceronian-Horatian
terms.

A partial retreat from the rigorous classical position
comes in the address 'To The Readers' of *Sejanus*
published in quarto in 1605:

First, if it be objected that what I publish is no true Poeme; in
the strict Lawes of *Time*. I confesse it: as also in the want of a
proper *Chorus*, whose Habite, and Moodes are such, and so
difficult, as not any, whome I have seene since the Auntients,
(no, not they who have most presently affected Lawes) have yet
come in the way off. Nor is it needful, or almost possible, in these

our Times, and to such Auditors, as commonly Things are presented, to observe the ould state, and splendour of *Dramatick Poemes*, with preservation of any popular delight. But of this I shall take more seasonable cause to speak: in my Observations upon *Horace* his *Art of Poetry*, which (with the Text translated) I intend, shortly to publish. In the meane time, if in truth of Argument, dignity of Persons, gravity and height of Elocution, fulnesse and frequencie of Sentence, I have discharg'd the other offices of a *Tragick* writer, let not the absence of these *Formes* be imputed to me, wherein I shall give you occasion hereafter (and without my boast) to thinke I could better prescribe, then omit the due use, for want of a convenient knowledge.  (vol. IV, p. 350)

The softening of the arrogant note declares that the critic is having to come to terms with his theatre. He has broken the rule of time and omitted the chorus. He admits to a kind of guilty ignorance as to what, essentially, the chorus is about, what exactly its 'moods' and 'habits' are intended to express. The ritualistic overtones of the Greek chorus, the attempt to apprehend in poetic terms a universal and mysterious fate, even the more obvious function of manipulating the audience's sympathies and so underscoring the ironies of the play, were no longer accessible experiences to Elizabethan readers or audiences any more than they are to us today. Thanks to closer acquaintance with Greek texts and Greek ideas, we may claim an intellectual acceptance of the chorus but it is doubtful whether a modern audience can experience its full emotional impact. In these our times we are disabled, as Jonson says, from observing 'the ould state and splendour of Dramatick Poemes'. But he can still satisfy those categories of the Aristotelian prescription for tragedy which demand a suitable plot (or argument) and appropriate characters, diction and thought (or *sententiae*). As a practitioner, a professional dramatist

44

relying on the support of audiences, he is aware that the Jacobean theatre is not the Greek theatre.

Having admitted to ignoring some of the 'laws' of classical tragedy, Jonson is concerned to provide a similar apology for dereliction of duty in respect of his comedy *Volpone*:

And though my catastrophe may, in the strict rigour of *comick* law, meet with censure, as turning back to my promise; I desire the learned, and charitable critick to have so much faith in me, to thinke it was done off industrie: For, with what ease I could have varied it, neerer his scale (but that I feare to boast my owne faculty) I could here insert. But my speciall ayme being to put the snaffle in their mouthes, that crie out, we never punish vice in our *enterludes, etc.* I tooke the more liberty; though not without some lines of example, drawne even in the ancients themselves, the goings out of whose *comœdies* are not alwaies ioyfull, but oft-times the bawdes, the servants, the rivals, yea, and the masters are mulcted: and fitly, it being the office of a *comick-Poet*, to imitate iustice, and to instruct to life, as well as puritie of language, or stirre up gentle affections...For the present (most reverenced *SISTERS*) as I have car'd to be thankefull for your affections past, and here made the understanding acquainted with some ground of your favours; let me not despaire their continuance, to the maturing of some worthier fruits; wherein, if my *MUSES* be true to me, I shall raise the despis'd head of *poetrie* again, and stripping her out of those rotten and bare rags, wherwith the Times have adulterated her form, restore her to her primitive habit, feature and maiesty, and render her worthy to be imbraced, and kist, of all the great and master-*spirits* of our world.   ('The Dedicatory Epistle', *Volpone*, Vol. v, pp. 20–1, folio 1616)

He was well aware that the comic trajectory should run from adversity to prosperity, as stated by Aristotle, maintained and emphasised for moral reasons through-out the Middle Ages and accepted by the neo-classical humanists. In *Volpone* the principal character is sentenced to 'lie in prison, cramp'd with irons' a punishment so severe that the play might seem to conclude on a discordant note with the hero suffering a fate close to that of the exiled Oedipus. Obviously Jonson felt that the play demanded such an ending and few would quarrel with him, while at the same time the gap between the classical definition of comedy and those ferocious reprisals which conclude and unify this 'beast play' was sufficiently obvious. He falls back on the old morality argument even using the by this time antique word 'enterludes' in order to justify his ending as a demonstration of vice being suitably punished. There is something strangely old-fashioned, deliberately myopic in Jonson's view, at this late date, 1607, that Poetry needed to have her despised head raised again, languishing as she is in 'rotten and bare rags'.

These perverse judgments may well be due to that vein of conceit which permeates Jonson's non-dramatic writing. He is determined to claim that he is, in the modern cant phrase, the greatest. In his prologues, as in that to *Volpone* his boasting verges on the indecent. Note, he says, how this play mixes 'profit with your pleasure'. Note too that it 'observeth the laws of time, place, persons', and note how all this was written in the short space of five weeks! Despite his peculiar creative genius, Jonson treats with the utmost reverence the laws of composition as interpreted from the writings of the ancients, and distrusts his own restless age.

In his commonplace book, called *Discoveries* he gives us a clear reflection of his critical predilections. In quoting, he tacitly expresses agreement with the sentiments of his authorities and so permits us to construct a fairly consistent picture of his critical views. He claims not to be a slavish imitator of the ancients and takes comfort in finding a similar sentiment expressed in the writings of the Spanish philosopher Juan Luis Vives, tutor to the Princess Mary and friend of Thomas More, who wrote:

Concerning the writings of great authors, 'tis much more profitable for literature to make a judgment than to agree with one authority alone and accept everything on trust from someone else. Only in the criticism and comment, let there be no curses, ill-will, bitterness, hastiness, insolence or scurrilous wit...So that it would seem that we could, if we applied our minds in the same way, make better pronouncements on life and nature than Aristotle, Plato or any of the ancients...As Seneca wisely says, those who have covered the ground before us are not our masters but our leaders.   (Vol. xi, p. 217)

Francis Bacon is later quoted to reinforce the view of Vives but he concludes *Discoveries* with a long extract from Daniel Heinsius, a Dutchman and the ruling critic of the age, who re-emphasised the primacy of the rules according to Scaliger – not surprising since he had been a pupil of Scaliger's son Joseph. The dogmatic tone of these pages declares their ancestry.

What might have been Jonson's most positive critical statement was presumably contained in the notes which he wrote for his translation of Horace's *Ars Poetica* and which were destroyed in his disastrous library fire in 1623. What we have left are the prologues and prefatory statements and the quotations in *Discoveries*. In effect, Jonson's views on the purpose, content and structure of drama are implicit in his plays rather than overtly stated in notes or essays.

Close analysis of the plays makes it clear that his adherence to 'rules' is less than one might expect from the kind of labels traditionally fixed on him. His 'humour' theory is an extension of Horatian decorum and yet the characters in *The Alchemist* or *Bartholomew Fair* have a closer family likeness to the comics in *Henry*

*IV* or *Measure for Measure* than to any of the creations of Plautus or Terence. Sixteenth-century Italian criticism, which gave France a dramatic formula lasting into the mid-eighteenth century, had considerably less influence on English practice. Whetstone, Sidney and a few others took a firm theoretical stand on it in the 1580s; Shakespeare ignored it; Jonson deferred to it in theory, which he knew mainly through his reading of Horace, Sidney and Heinsius. The firm Scaligerian views of the latter are passed on to Dryden through Jonson, for whom, it must be remembered, Dryden had the very highest respect. Although Jonson's critical writing is small in quantity, it achieves added importance in the Restoration period through his lasting reputation as one of the giants of olden times.

# 3

# French neo-classicism

Meanwhile, in France the ideas of Scaliger and Castelvetro became part of the common currency of literary
discussion and debate. As André de Rivandeau says in
1566 – and one sympathises with his tone while deplor-
ing his lack of devotion to his books – he who wants to
read something on tragedy is recommended 'to a mighty
tome made by one Scaliger of which so far I've seen only
the title'.[1] By 1572 Jean de la Taille in his preface to *Saül
le furieux* established the essential nature of the unities of
time and place in tragedy, that 'most elegant, excellent
and splendid' kind of poetry. Seven years later, however,
Pierre de Laudun in his *Art poëtique françois* gives five
reasons, and assures his reader he has a thousand others
if he had time to state them, why the action of a tragedy
cannot be confined to one day. Just as Castelvetro argues
that adherence to a narrow time bracket helps the
illusion, relates the action more closely to real life, so de
Laudun argues that the illusion cannot be maintained if
too many incidents are packed into one day, or,
alternatively, if one day is the limit, the poem will be bare,
graceless, devoid of matter.[2] Already the debate is joined,
the terms of which will become familiar as critics and
playwrights worry over the demands of illusion, of
'vraisemblance' and 'bienséance'. By 1628 Francois

[1] Quoted by H. W. Lawton in *Handbook of French Renaissance Dramatic
Theory*.
[2] Lawton, *French Renaissance Dramatic Theory*, p. 99.

Ogier in the preface to *Tyr et Sidon* by Jean de Schelandre comes out in favour of the moderns against the ancients. *Vraisemblance* is outraged by the compression of events into one day. By this standard, far too much happens in *Oedipus Rex*. In order to fill in the action, the ancients have to introduce messengers and their long tales are a bore. Poetry, in particular theatre poetry, is meant for pleasure and diversion and if these aims are to be achieved, the unity of time must be ignored. What was good for the Greeks and Romans is not necessarily good for today. 'One must examine and consider these methods in the light of the circumstances of the time, the place and the people for whom they have been composed.'[3] It is a good thing, he goes on, that the Italians introduced tragi-comedy so that we can have the light relief of comedy mixed in with tragedy instead of having to follow a sombre tragedy by a satyr play, as the Greeks felt compelled to do:

For to say that it is indecorous to have appear in one play the same people, dealing at one moment with serious important and tragic affairs and immediately afterwards with idle common and comic business is to ignore the condition of the life of men whose days and hours are often a mingling of laughter and tears, happiness and grief, according as they are moved by good or ill fortune.[4]

In any case, Euripides' *Cyclops* is in fact a tragi-comedy with raillery and wine-bibbing on the one hand and the rage of the blinded Polyphemus on the other. 'So the thing is old, though the name (tragi-comedy) be new.'[5] So much for the adherence to the 'rules' on the part of French writers in the early seventeenth century. In the same year that Ogier was writing, Alexandre Hardy completed the publication of his five volumes of extant

---

[3] Ibid. p. 115.
[4] Lawton, *French Renaissance Dramatic Theory*, p. 126.
[5] Ibid. p. 126.

plays, thirty-four in all, of which fourteen are designated tragi-comedies.[6]

Two years later, in 1630, Jean Chapelain (1595–1674) wrote his letter to a would-be playwright, Antoine Godeau, which has come to be known as the *Letter Concerning The Twenty-four Hour Rule*.[7] In itself the letter might have been simply another document in the debate about the unities which as we have seen had been flourishing in France for the previous sixty years. Its writer however was destined to become an arbiter with more than ordinary powers when he was elected a member of the newly founded French Academy and gained the confidence of Richelieu who, in due course, instructed him to prepare the formal report on Corneille's *Le Cid*. Chapelain's case for the twenty-four hour rule rests on the argument that in poetry the imitation should be so perfect that there appears to be no difference between the thing imitated and the imitation. Only thus can the conviction of truth and presence offered by the imitation achieve the end of poetry, namely, the purging of unruly passions. The spectator must be made to believe what he sees, and never doubt its 'reality'. The ancients reckoned that a twenty-four hour bracket was the maximum permissible to achieve this degree of probability in the theatre.

Chapelain's correspondent has asked whether a play can contain more than one action and to this he is, consistently, given the answer that a single action is enough. To achieve this unity of action, the ancients used narrators and messengers, and chose the moment of crisis for presentation on the stage. Then there is the matter of illusion. Of course the spectator knows that the ongoings on the stage are make-believe but he must

---

[6] G. Brereton, *French Tragic Drama in the 16th and 17th Centuries*, pp. 59 and 67.

[7] Reprinted in Jean Chapelain, *Opuscules critiques* with an introduction by Alfred C. Hunter.

believe in them for all that. If he goes to the theatre in a sceptical frame of mind, he abuses the whole purpose of poetry and voluntarily loses the benefit he could gain from it. On the question of stage time to be represented, there is a considerable difference between one day and ten years and the imagination can accept the events of twenty-four hours being portrayed in three hours but not events spread over ten years. Since temporal limitations are thus demanded by the reason, so also are spatial. The events of ten years would demand changes in location which the eye would find itself unable to accept.

As to the argument that liberation from the twenty-four hour rule would add to the pleasure of the theatre – assuming that the current function of the theatre is to provide pleasure – both propositions must be denied. If contemporary taste has reduced the theatre to a mere vehicle for pleasure, all the more reason to lead poetry back to its proper function. We see nowadays the arts and sciences regaining their former glory after the long Gothic withdrawal. If the ancient virtues are to be imitated in all manner of ways, would one want to ignore the theatre and hold it alone in a state of barbarism? Furthermore, if the sole end of the theatre is in fact pleasure, these 'improvements' (abolition of time–place rules) would disgust those people who could discriminate false pleasures from genuine ones. It is certain that theatrical pleasure stems from sound structure and credibility, matters in which the ancients put their trust although there are those today who would destroy them. The letter concludes by touching on a theme which we shall hear frequently debated in English Restoration criticism, whether blank verse or rhyme be most suited to dramatic dialogue. Consistent with his literal, representational interpretation of mimesis, Chapelain comes down emphatically in support of blank verse or prose.

Chapelain's further thoughts on dramatic theory are to be found in the first draft of *The Views of the French Academy concerning the Observations made on the tragicomedy 'Le Cid'*. Scudéry, having published his observations on the play, the Academy asked Chapelain to prepare a reply which was submitted to the members and to Richelieu who apparently returned it for re-writing before publication in 1638. According to Hunter this second version fails to give in an undiluted form 'either the opinions or the language of Chapelain'.[8] The following summary and comments are based on the first version as printed in *Opuscules critiques*.

Criticism, says Chapelain, clearly answering in advance any accusation of personal animus against Corneille, is a good thing provided it be not the product of malignity or jealousy and a play like *Le Cid*, which has attracted a deal of attention, merits this examination by the Academy. Views may differ as to the function of poetry, whether it should provide pleasure or profit, but merely to give pleasure in itself is not enough if the work fails to satisfy reason by lacking regularity, by not conforming with the rules. In this respect *Le Cid* is to be condemned because its plot does not satisfy reason and overpasses the bounds of probability. As far as we interpret the views of Aristotle on probability, he recognised two types: the first the common kind which includes things that happen in ordinary life to men, according to their circumstances, ages, characters and emotions as when it is probable or reasonable that a merchant looks for profit, a child is imprudent, a coward dodges danger; then there is the out-of-the-ordinary kind of probability which covers things that seldom happen and go beyond ordinary day-to-day expectations, as when a clever knave is swindled or a powerful tyrant is overthrown. In this category

[8] Chapelain, *Opuscules critiques*, p. 153.

come those accidents which take one by surprise and one says they are by chance, but still they should be the product of a chain of circumstances, which happens in the ordinary run of things. Aristotle is concerned with the probable rather than with the true in the sense of 'that which has happened' because the probable in epic and drama provides that instruction which is their aim. The 'true' could throw up events so strange and incredible that an audience would not believe them and would refuse to be persuaded.

The most essential element in establishing probability is that each person acts in conformity with the character which has been given him and this is the more important because the marvellous which is necessary to hold attention through giving pleasure (without pleasure there can be no profit) must be a part of this probability, this totally acceptable situation. This is no easy task, to reconcile the probable and the marvellous and so writers often present a version of the marvellous which is patently false and therefore improbable. The marvellous becomes the monstrous and this is the fault in *Le Cid* where there is neither ordinary probability nor extraordinary probability. The marvellous which should give the audience profit and instruction tends instead towards the monstrous and so fills them with indignation and horror.

The stricture (maintained by Scudéry) that Corneille did wrong in choosing a subject rooted in history and then tampering with the historical facts is not maintained. The poet has every justification for altering the facts of history provided he holds on to the rule of probability. Poetry is entitled to correct the wickednesses of history, making them appear good for the greater benefit of the public. The real fault is that too much happens too quickly in *Le Cid* and what happens goes beyond the bounds of credibility. On the matter of time,

Corneille might have been wiser to follow his Spanish original and break the twenty-four hour rule. But the most serious defect in the play is the breach of decorum exemplified in the portrayal of Chimène. She betrays her natural duty in favour of her passion and is in every sense a scandalous woman. And so the charges against *Le Cid* are summed up: the subject is defective; the denouement is unworthy; the plot is loaded with superfluous episodes; the laws of decorum are not everywhere observed.

In these two statements – the letter on the twenty-four hour rule and the commentary on *Le Cid* – Chapelain summarises the principal criteria which were to be relevant in the making of value judgments on dramatic poetry for the rest of the century. The primary essential is probability: what is presented must be seen to be likely and must be reasonably accepted as such. A dash of the marvellous is however necessary to give the pleasurable topping-up to a play so that audiences will respond and thereby be instructed. The instruction must accord with the accepted social code of the age and with a certain ideal standard of morality. Poetry is a matter of rhetoric, the manipulation of an audience's emotions for moral ends, and so becomes identified with purposes which are unpoetic in their intention and is judged by norms existing outside of itself. Poetic imitation is identified with social and moral conformity; Chimène does not conform, so she is a bad imitation. Seventeenth-century critics, taking their cue from the Italian philosophers of the previous age, were unwilling to grant poetry its own autonomy.

Out of this there develops a double standard of evaluation. Certain events are not acceptable because they are not naturalistic; e.g. it is absurd that Rodrigue should, unaccompanied, enter the house the master of which he has just killed, go straight to the daughter's

55

apartment and meet not a single servant to stop him on the way.[9] On the other hand, certain events are not acceptable not because they could not have happened, but because if they were related as having happened, they would be deemed indecorous, i.e. not in accordance with the ideal code of conduct as laid down at the time. Into this category falls Chimène's continuing love for her father's murderer and her apparent willingness to marry him. Naturalism, the closest possible identification between reality and fiction, is invoked in order to persuade an audience that these things as portrayed are, in a general sense, 'true'. On the other hand, the purpose of the persuasion is to instruct, to teach good morality, to present an idealised picture of human conduct. The problem of compatability between these two desirable properties of drama lives on even as far as the reflections of Samuel Johnson a century later.

By the time the *Views of the French Academy* was published, the period of uncertainty and controversy over the rules and the accepted structure of a play was virtually over in France. Subsequent writing reiterates, systematises and confirms what should be done even although playwrights and audiences frequently collaborated in the presentation of examples which adhered only remotely to the official formula. For an example of an elaborate, sustained and persuasive thesis on the nature and practice of drama one might profitably turn to the work of François Hédelin (1604–1676) later L'Abbé D'Aubignac, and so commonly referred to as D'Aubignac.

D'Aubignac was born in Paris, the son of a barrister and grandson of a surgeon. After a period in his father's profession he took orders and came to the notice of Richelieu, who made him tutor to one of his nephews, the Duc de Fronsac, through whom he obtained the abbacies

[9] Chapelain, *Opuscules critiques*, p. 181.

of Aubignac and Mainac. For the last thirty years of his
life he devoted himself to literature, becoming particularly concerned with the idea of establishing a theatre
firmly based on classical principles. At Richelieu's suggestion he began in 1640 a work which appeared seventeen
years later entitled *Dramatic Practice* (*La Pratique du
théâtre*) with the extended sub-title: 'Very necessary work
for those who wish to apply themselves to the composition of dramatic poems, or who recite them in public or
who enjoy their performance'.

In his opening chapter D'Aubignac puts drama firmly
in its place as a moral teacher: virtue must be rewarded,
or at least praised. Even the insensitive mob will learn
from drama that fortune's favours do not bring true
happiness. The old French theatre was 'like an exhumed
corpse, hideous, deformed, without strength and almost
without movement' but now, thanks to the Cardinal and
the example of Euripides and Terence, things are on the
mend:[10]

There is a difference between knowledge of the rules of an art
and their application...Much has been said about the value of
drama; its origin, its development, its definition, its types, unity
of action, limit of time, beauty of the incidents, the thoughts,
characters, language and a thousand other such things in
general which I call the theory of the theatre. But as for
observations which must be made on these fundamental rules,
as the skill in arranging the incidents, the linking of time and
place, continuity of action, linking of scenes, spacing of the acts
and a hundred other details, I don't remember anything
written by the ancients or moderns. This is what I call the
practice of the theatre. Many of our moderns do not know the
ancient plays or have neglected to observe their finer points.
Certainly no one will be an expert on the theatre without the
help of the ancients and a knowledge of their works. (Book I,
ch. 3)

[10] Authors' translations from F. D'Aubignac, *La Pratique du théâtre*
(1715).

The practice of the theatre is what concerns D'Aubignac, a practice still firmly embedded in classical precept, but this precept, although doubtless stated by Aristotle, has in fact its origins in reason (Book I, ch. 4). The action of a play must be clearly motivated, step by step. This is called 'maintaining *couleur*'. The young writer must still read his Aristotle and Horace and study their commentators including Castelvetro, Vida, Heinsius, Vossius and so on. Let him remember that Scaliger alone said more than all the others did but that all of them are important (Book I, ch. 5).

In Book II D'Aubignac, introducing the idea of verisimilitude, pleads for a firmly structured logical action – a demonstration of cause and effect in dramatic terms. The truth, he says, is not proper matter for the theatre because many true happenings should not be seen or cannot be represented. Nor is the 'possible' appropriate for the theatre:

In a word, verisimilitude is the very heart of the dramatic poem. Without verisimilitude, nothing reasonable can be said or done on the stage.
It is a generally accepted maxim that truth [le Vrai] is not the material of the theatre for there are many true things which cannot be looked upon and many which cannot be acted...It is true for instance that Nero had his mother strangled and her inside opened up so that he could see where he had been carried for nine months before his birth, but this kind of barbarity, acceptable to the man who carried it out, would not only be horrible to those who might see it, but even incredible.
That which is possible is also not in itself suitable material for drama. There are plenty of things which could happen which would be ridiculous and incredible if they were performed. A man can die suddenly; it often happens, but it would make a fool of everybody, if, in order to unravel the plot of a play, a rival were to die of apoplexy as if it were a natural and common

ailment. To get away with it, you would need a deal of ingenious preparation. It's possible for a man to be struck dead by lightning but it would be a poor piece of plotting for the poet thus to get rid of a lover whom he had used in order to complicate his comedy.

So there is nothing but verisimilitude for the establishment, maintenance and completion of a play. This does not mean that true events or possible events are banished from the theatre, but such events can get into the play only in so far as they possess verisimilitude. So it will be necessary to remove or alter any circumstances which don't have this quality; equally, whatever is presented on the stage must bear the mark of verisimilitude. (Book III, ch. 2)

This verisimilitude must extend to the character in his context:

When a King makes a speech on the stage, he must speak like a King and it is the display of this impregnable dignity which provides verisimilitude, unless there is some reason for dispensing with this circumstance, as it might be, for instance, if the King were in disguise. I further maintain that this King whose speech from the stage accords with his dignity is doubtless in some particular place where he will make these pronouncements. So the stage must provide a representation of the place where he is, for there are things which one cannot speak with an air of verisimilitude in certain places. So also will it be necessary to represent and make clear the time when he speaks for it will often be necessary to alter the tone of discourse to suit the time. A Prince before battle will speak very differently from the same man after a battle which he has either won or lost. To maintain this verisimilitude in the varied circumstances of dramatic action, it is essential to know the rules and apply them; for they teach only one thing, namely, how to give verisimilitude to all aspects of the action when they are presented on the stage so as to give a wholly integrated and acceptable performance. (Book II, ch. 2)

The position is clear enough. There must be dramatic

illusion, the sense of looking in through the fourth wall – 'as if no one were looking at them (the actors)' is D'Aubignac's phrase. Horatian decorum is put to the service of verisimilitude. Kings must talk in a dignified manner at a certain time in a certain place and so, by being consistent, they are the more credible; they attain to that verisimilitude which, in accordance with the rules, is the aim of an integrated and acceptable performance.

D'Aubignac is however aware that dramatic verisimilitude is a convention in its own right. Even common sense and natural reason are not in themselves capable of assessing this quality of verisimilitude:

On this matter, it has been said that common sense and natural reason are adequate for forming a sound judgment. I agree, but this common sense must be a common sense trained to recognize both the aims and intentions of the theatre and the means employed to achieve these ends. Suppose for example a man of sound common sense had never seen a play and had never heard anyone talk about the theatre, it's quite certain he would not know whether the actors were real Kings and Princes or mere shadows and when he understood that all this was only a show, a bit of guising, he would be incapable of judging either the beauties or the defects of the play. Obviously he'd have to see several plays and think about them in order to recognize whether or not they had the quality of verisimilitude. Yes, indeed, in order to be a good judge of drama one must ensure that as well as having natural good sense, one must be knowledgeable about the mimetic medium which writers have been concerned to use in order to present a certain action and about the methods through which verisimilitude can be maintained in every aspect of this form of living portraiture. Such knowledge can only be acquired as a consequence of a lengthy series of observations made over a long period and by a large number of people.   (Book II, ch. 2)

Even experts can be caught out:

60

It's an odd thing, and true for all that, but I've known students of the drama read or see a play several times without noticing the time-bracket, or the location, or the most important parts of the action so as to reveal the quality of verisimilitude. Heinsius, usually a man of sound scholarship (he wrote down for us the art of composing tragedy) made so monstrous a howler as to believe that Plautus's *Amphitryon* covered nine months instead of eight hours; or at most it is contained within the time between midnight and mid-day of the same day.   (Book II, ch. 2)

In the third and fourth chapters of Book II D'Aubignac discusses structure in practical and moderate terms. A dramatist must select his incidents, otherwise there would be confusion and a breakdown of verisimilitude. If the chosen story contains too many incidents, the poet must cut some out; if too few, he must invent some. (Book II, ch. 3) The play must be structured as a whole. If the poet stopped the action at the end of the second act and made no indication of what was to follow, the audience would reasonably think the play had finished.

Opposing any modern dissidence, D'Aubignac goes on to confound the ignorant and undiscerning who think that the unity of place spoils the beauty of the incidents. With disarming nonchalance, he suggests that Aristotle said nothing about the unity of place because the rule was too well known in his time to need special mention. A voyage from France to Denmark cannot possibly be symbolised by three notes on a violin or the drawing of a curtain (Book II, ch. 6). You may however change the set if you establish adequate 'couleur', i.e. motivation. An empty castle can be furnished, set on fire and destroyed so as to reveal a sea-fight in the distance, but the plot must be strong enough to justify all this. Every appearance of an actor on the stage must likewise be adequately justified.

The seventh chapter is devoted to the unity of time

61                              3-2

which D'Aubignac considers to be the most controversial
subject of the age:

We must consider the dramatic poem as having two sorts of
time, each of which has its own appropriate duration. First is the
actual length of the performance...the extent of this period of
time cannot be other than the extent of the patience of the
audience. The audience must not be bored or fatigued...it also
must not be so short that the audience feels insufficiently
entertained.   (Book II, ch. 7)

So, he goes on, experience teaches us that plays cannot
last more than three hours, about 1500 lines of text. The
other duration is that of the action represented, in so far
as it is considered as real. This has been the subject of
many different opinions:

I have actually seen plays so disordered that in the first act a
prince was married, in the second, his son, the hero, was born;
in the third the young prince appeared quite grown up; in the
fourth made love and conquests; in the fifth married a princess,
who obviously had only been born since the opening of the play,
and hadn't even been spoken of.   (Book II, ch. 7)

After a long exhausting discussion he comes round to
Castelvetro's position that as far as possible real time and
dramatic time should coincide. The incidents must be
arranged with ingenious skill and must appear natural
in the course of the action, and not offend against
vraisemblance.

Having disposed of the problem of time, D'Aubignac
moves on to consider those aspects of the play to which
William Archer two centuries later applied the labels
'Point of Attack', 'Complication' and 'Catastrophe'.
When considering the preparation of incidents:

some will say that if the incidents must be prepared a long time
before they happen, they will doubtless be foreseen and they
will not cause the surprise on which their success depends; the

audience will have no pleasure and the dramatist no glory. (Book II, ch. 8)

The answer is to prepare for the incidents, lay down logical lines of development, without anticipating them or allowing the audience to guess what is going to happen before it actually happens. Preparation must mean no more than it says and the dramatist must find situations so contrived in their outcome as to fully justify the preparations.

Although he expresses himself obliquely, often tortuously and at great length, D'Aubignac is clear about the difference between art and life in this context. The theatre is concerned with a structured world, 'a special world in which everything is circumscribed by the ideas and scope of the action, a world which has no contact with the world outside except in so far as the dramatist by his skill establishes recognition' (Book II, ch. 8).

An insistence on form, on logical structure, runs through D'Aubignac's essay. The catastrophe should be prepared for but should be surprising when it comes and should arise out of the heart of the action, not through divine intervention (Book II, ch. 9). Audiences are accommodating in so far as they concern themselves only with what is happening in front of them, and are satisfied with the argument as stated without trying to look ahead, unless the pointers are too obvious. In short, they allow themselves to be deceived by the skill of the dramatist. They should however feel satisfied that the end of the play is its proper end; nothing should remain which they ought to know or might want to hear. On the other hand, we want no useless speeches or superfluous action at the conclusion of the play (Book II, ch. 8).

In endeavouring to define tragedy and comedy, D'Aubignac leans heavily on Scaliger:

Tragedies deal with princes; they are full of troubles, suspicion, dissension, rebellion, war, murder, violent passions and great events. They need not have an unhappy ending. A play is called a tragedy, not because of the catastrophe but because of the incidents and characters. Comedies depict the actions of the people and one sees in them nothing but the debauchery of the young, the tricks of slaves, the charms of loose women, prostitutes, love affairs, jokes, marriages and other happenings of everyday life. (Book II, ch. 10)

Comedy he goes on is at a low ebb in France. Only farce and insolent buffoonery are offered, works unworthy to be classed as plays, 'without art, without divisions, without sense, only acceptable to knaves and fools'. Adaptations and imitations of the ancient comedy have fared no better than attempts to acclimatise Italian *commedia dell' arte*. Significantly enough, *La Pratique du théâtre* was published one year before Molière brought his company to Court and began, first through farce and then in genuine comedies, to establish that reputation which has given him a permanent place beside Terence and Plautus.

D'Aubignac is not quite so despondent about tragedy. The French character, he thinks, is heroic and serious and so the French public is more inclined to regard the adventures of heroes sympathetically. Stories of horror and extraordinary cruelty are no longer acceptable, nor, he says in an earlier chapter (Book II, ch. 1) are those recitals of kings in misery or noble families cast down, since the French nation has too much respect for their kings and princes to view such horrors with equanimity. This was good enough for democratic Athens but they order things differently in seventeenth-century France. He objects to the use of the term 'tragi-comedies' (Book II, ch. 10). Tragedies are still tragedies, no matter if they have a happy ending, so long as they depict the fortunes of the great.

The third book of *La Pratique* concentrates on technical details many of which D'Aubignac has already touched on. Prologues should not reveal the plot. Corneille is careful never to do this (Book III, ch. 1). It is interesting to note that several complimentary references to Corneille in this book were later found to be deleted from D'Aubignac's own copy of *La Pratique*; such were the pressures and antipathies of artistic polemic in the Paris of these days.[11] Some Greek prologues, he continues, introduced gods who actually forecast the end of the play and so ruined it. His references to the choric odes suggest that, as in the case of Jonson, he was unable to appreciate their real purpose. They are no more than musical interludes which can be removed without loss to the play. He returns in chapter two to his favourite topic of structure: 'The greatest skill of the dramatist lies in arranging well the incidents of his story'. Episodes must be appropriate and consistent, drawn from the heart of the theme, and they must not be too long. There should be five acts, the end of each act being signalised by a temporary cessation of all action. He quarrels with Aristotle for suggesting that some prior incidents necessary for a full understanding of the story may be referred to (e.g. in the prologue) without necessarily being presented as part of the action. Everything should be brought into the action: this is what good construction is about.[12]

Corneille is very good at this for in his arrangement of acts and scenes he places incidents so appropriately that moments of

---

[11] For details of the quarrel see *Le Théâtre et Le Public à Paris sous Louis XIV 1659–1715* by Pierre Mélèse, pp. 314–20.

[12] D'Aubignac, *La Pratique*.

passion are brilliantly illuminated where other writers might so arrange incidents as to lose all their beauty. (Book III, ch. 5)

Thus must the young writer consider the elements of his story, the structuring of his acts and scenes to build up his big moments, and thirdly, his dialogue. Here he must endeavour to cultivate and improve what nature has given him and study the masters. He must envisage his play as a whole before he starts to write it down. 'He who knows the whole will take good care of the parts.' And he must take pains to make his opening 'éclatante' either in the number or majesty of the actors or by a grand spectacle or an extraordinary narration.

As we struggle through D'Aubignac's turgid prose, time and again we come across those percipient comments which reveal his genuine understanding of the theatre as he knew it and as he wanted it to be in the particular conditions of his country at this time. Despite his reputation even in his own day as a pedant, his approach endeavours to remove dramatic theory from the world of the grammarians and philosophers and put it where it belongs, in the dramatist's study and in the playhouse. 'He is in effect a mediocre, if tireless thinker; but he is often a wise observer' wrote his fellow country-man, C. Arnaud, in 1888.[13] Certainly dramatic criticism would have been the loser if he had yielded to his first temptation to burn the manuscript of *La Pratique* after the death of Richelieu. Friends urged him to publish, and seven years after publication, in 1664, he was sufficiently pleased with his work to write: 'The only people who have found fault with *La Pratique* are fools'. Among the fools was Pierre Corneille, who could find little that pleased him in the book.

By the time Corneille (1606–1684) published his *Three*

---

[13] *Les Théories dramatiques au* XVII$^e$ *siècle – Étude sur L'Abbé D'Aubignac*, C. Arnaud, 1888.

*Discourses* in 1660, he was the experienced author of twenty-two plays, and despite the prejudice, polemic and critical perversity of many of his compatriots, he was the acknowledged master of the French stage. He may well have been stung into making this formal defence of his principles by some remarks of D'Aubignac which he found less than appreciative. If so, we have D'Aubignac to thank for the appearance of a work which the actor-director of our own age, Jean Louis Barrault, is reputed to include among the five books of essential reading for aspiring actors.[14] The first essay, 'On the Utility and Parts of the Dramatic Poem', starts boldly with a quotation from Aristotle applied directly to his own work:[15]

Although, according to Aristotle, the sole end of drama is to please the audience and although the greater part of these my plays have given pleasure, I am nonetheless ready to admit that many of them have failed to achieve the purpose of art. 'We do not claim,' says Aristotle, 'that this form of poetry gives us every kind of pleasure, but only that which is proper to it'; and to find this pleasure which is proper to it and to give this pleasure to the audience, we must follow the precepts of art and please them in accordance with the rules. It is established that there are rules, since we are dealing with an art, but it is not established what the rules are. One agrees about the name without agreeing about the thing; one concurs in the words only to contest their meaning. Unity of action, place and time must be observed, that is certain. But it is not easy to know what this unity of action is, or how far we are permitted to stretch the unities of time and place. (p. 317)

He quotes *The Poetics*, chapter xv referring to the poet's treatment of his subject in accordance with the probable

---

[14] Quoted by L. R. Chambers in *Aspects of Drama and the Theatre*, Sidney U.P., 1965, p. 138.

[15] Quotations are translated from *Œuvres complètes de Pierre Corneille*, vol. v.

and the necessary, but what, he asks, are these things? Does the subject of tragedy have to be likely or probable (*vraisemblable*)? Historical events are likely in so far as they are historical and some legends are likely because they are traditionally accepted. Classical tragedy concentrates on a few families because events worthy of tragedy can only happen in a limited number of families. The utility of the dramatic poem is his next consideration:

I proposed at the beginning of this essay that dramatic poetry has for its aim nothing but the pleasure of the audience. I am not trying to contradict those who would ennoble the art by claiming it should give instruction as well as pleasure...It is true that Aristotle in the whole of *The Poetics* never once uses the word (utility) and that he attributes the origin of poetry to be the pleasure we take in seeing an imitation of the actions of men...but it is no less true that Horace tells us that we will fail to please everyone if we do not include instruction, and that grave and serious people, old men and upholders of virtue, will be bored if they find no profit. So although instruction comes in the guise of delight, it is nonetheless essential. (*Œuvres complètes*, pp. 318–19)

There are four kinds of utility or instruction to be had from drama, the fourth applying only to tragedy:

The first kind of utility or instruction consists in *sententiae* and moral apothegms which one can scatter more or less all through the play. But this method should be used in moderation; such *sententiae* should really be part of a general discourse and should hardly ever be introduced when a character is speaking in an impassioned way or when he is being answered by another character...

The second kind of instruction consists in the unaffected presentation of vices and virtues. When well done, when the characteristics of vice and virtue are so clearly defined that there can be no confusion between them, such presentation will always be effective. Virtue is always loved even when it leads to misery, and vice is always hated even when triumphant. The ancients accepted such representation, without concerning themselves about rewarding virtue or punishing vice. (pp. 319–20)

The third kind of instruction is a reinforcement of the second. Despite classical precedent, it is better nowadays to punish the wicked and reward the good at the end of your play:

It is clear that we cannot see a good character on the stage without wishing his good fortune and without being concerned about his miseries. This means that when he is beaten by misfortune we leave the play overcome by chagrin and a kind of indignation against both authors and actors: but when the outcome fulfills our desires and virtue emerges triumphant, we quit the theatre happy, wholly satisfied with the work and with those who have presented it. The happy success of virtue in spite of perils and crosses moves us to embrace it: and the lamentable success of crime or injustice results in increasing our natural horror of it. (p. 321)

There is another kind of utility centred on the alleged purgation of the passions through pity and fear, 'catharsis', but that will be dealt with later. The parts of the dramatic poem as outlined by Aristotle are the subject (*mythos*), the characterisation, which is a matter of ethics, the diction which is a matter of grammar, and music and decoration which are strictly speaking not the concern of the poet. Tragedy is not essentially defined by reference to people of high esteem nor is comedy solely the province of low characters. Kings or princes may get themselves into situations where there is no threat to life, but can you call that tragedy merely because kings and princes are involved? A love interest by itself cannot be tragic. You can have heroic, i.e. aristocratic, comedy. Tragedy is concerned with an action which is illustrious, extraordinary, serious and complete and should involve peril of life, loss of state or banishment. There are crimes in tragedy but these crimes are committed by people possessed of such greatness of soul (*grandeur d'âme*) that even while we find the deeds hateful, we are consumed with admiration for the source from which they spring. Having come close to seizing on an important truth regarding the nature of tragic sublimity, Corneille tends to weaken his argument by quoting his own comedy, *Le Menteur*, where the talent for grandiose lying is shown to be a vice but a vice beyond the ability of fools.

He seems to rest content at this point with taking *grandeur* to mean simply larger than life and quotes Robortello and Castelvetro in support of his argument.

Characters in our play should be good unless it is our particular purpose to show criminals in action. They should be suited to their part in the play; if they have historical prototypes, these should be imitated, and they should be consistent. Like so many critics before him, Corneille questions why Aristotle should apparently place action before character. Surely, he argues, character is not only the motivation of action, it also motivates the reasoning behind the action. A man of good will acts and reasons in character as does a bad man and both give voice to maxims of morality or immorality in accordance with their diverse characters. Tragedy can dispense with the maxims but not with character which lies behind the action, and action is the soul of tragedy. So when Aristotle talks of tragedy without character, he means that kind of tragedy wherein the actors simply state what they intend to do (their 'sentiments') without expanding on their action by moral or political argumentation. 'I say again, it is absolutely impossible to write a play where the actors are neither good nor bad, neither prudent nor imprudent.' Furthermore, the poet cannot simply make statements about this, that or the other as if he were an orator; he has to work through his characters; he himself never speaks. Concluding this first essay, Corneille has a cursory word on diction and scenery and leaves us slightly shattered by the comment that music is useful to drown the noise of the machines.

The second essay is specifically about tragedy and the manner of treating it in accordance with the probable or the necessary. As well as the three 'utilities' already discussed, tragedy has this special one that by pity and fear it purges like passions. Corneille now accuses Aristotle of explaining pity, but not fear, so, he reckons, we must engage in some conjectural expansion of the Aristotelian concept. Aristotle can be deemed to say: 'We pity those who suffer undeservedly and we fear lest we do too.' Thus, we pity *them* on the stage but we fear for *us* in the audience. The Greek princes are essentially men like other people moved by ambition, love, hate, vengeance and if princes fall a victim to these passions in excess, so too will we. So we must keep a rein on our passions. Now he examines Aristotle's presentation of the nature of the tragic hero:[16]

It remains then to find a man between these two extremes by choosing a man who is neither entirely good nor entirely wicked and who by some fault or human weakness falls into a misfortune which he does not deserve. Aristotle gives as examples Oedipus and Thyestes and here I frankly cannot understand his thought. The first does not appear to me to commit a crime, even although he kills his father, because he does not recognise him and because he merely puts up a spirited defence of his right of passage against an unknown person who attacks with superior numbers. (p. 340)

As for Thyestes, he is an even more complicated case. If he is incestuous, then the audience being themselves

[16] Corneille, *Œuvres.*

71

incapable of such enormity will not fear for themselves since Thyestes does not resemble them. Or, is he the victim of his own credence, of trusting his brother-in-law? In this case we will pity him and perhaps have some fear for ourselves but only in so far as we will begin to suspect the virtue inherent in trustworthiness and this would not have a moral application. He concludes: 'If the passions are indeed purged in tragedy, it is done in the way I explain. But I doubt if it ever happens, even in the case of those passions which have the conditions Aristotle demands.' (p. 340) In *Le Cid* Rodrigue and Chimène are unfortunate because they are impassioned. They are indeed pitiful and the audience weeps for them, but does the audience feel any fear?

This pity ought to inspire in us a fear of falling into like misfortune and purge in us this superfluity of amorousness the like of which causes their misery and makes us pity them – but I doubt if it does fill us with fear or purge us of excessive passions. I greatly fear that Aristotle's reasoning on this point is merely a fine concept which in truth never gains its effect.   (p. 341)

Some people, says Corneille, think that Aristotle may have been trying to submit a moral argument to counter Plato's condemnation of the poets but the validity of the moral argument is hard to find when we note that in his plays, unlike ours, the wicked are not punished nor are the good always rewarded. Apart from maxims and moral discourses which in any case he did not consider essential, Aristotle failed to find a genuine purpose in tragedy so he substituted one which may be illusory. Robortello found the Aristotelian conditions only in *Oedipus*. So it may be that Aristotle's conception of catharsis is an ideal but not part of a necessary prescription. And with his usual charming suavity Corneille adds that his age has seen these conditions fully satisfied only in *Le Cid*.

Referring back to the Aristotelian heroic type, he objects to the exclusion of totally virtuous people from the principal role in tragedy. Such a ruling banishes martyrs, but his own Polyeucte, Héraclius, and Nicomède have been satisfactory heroes. Only Polyeucte is a true martyr suffering death, but all three are the objects of oppression through no fault of their own, therefore we cannot identify a fault demanding correction in them or in ourselves. Some crimes may excite a sympathetic chord in the audience, not because they themselves would commit them, for they are grander, more enormous, more dreadful crimes than the audience would ever be in a position to commit, but they might recognise the possibility of their being involved in a somewhat similar if less grandiose misfortune. He instances – they are pretty far fetched instances – the plight of Rodogune and of Cléopatre.

Now comes the Corneillian solution to the problem of Aristotelian catharsis. If moral purging is what we are after, then fear is the necessary emotion which must be aroused in us, but we do not need pity. We fear for ourselves; we show pity for the characters. Pity by itself does not purge, but fear does. The two together are not necessary as long as we accept that pity or compassion unaccompanied by fear does not purge us of anything. So Aristotle would not refuse his suffrage to the inclusion of events arousing either pity or fear (but not necessarily both). Once again *Oedipus* is the reference point. We do not in the normal run of things expect to marry our mother or kill our father so we have no fear for ourselves in the course of our dramatic engagement with *Oedipus*. We do however pity him. If he has any fault which we might conceivably share, it could be too much curiosity

73

about the future and having recourse to fortune tellers. The real fault in *Oedipus* lies however at the door of Jocasta and Laius and these events lie outside the play. So we may have pity or we may have fear and we may even have pity roused by one character and fear by another. In the perfect situation, pity and fear are excited by the action of one and the same man, as Rodrigue in *Le Cid* and Placide in *Théodore*. The suffering of a totally good man or the punishment of a totally bad man may have exemplary value, although we are aware that such situations did not enter into Aristotle's assessment of the function of tragedy.

Corneille, using his own plays as examples, is confirming in theory what his plays demonstrate in practice, that he has moved away from the sixteenth-century theorists (and from D'Aubignac) by being less concerned about the moral, exemplary aspect of drama (summed up in the idea of fear – fear for the punishment that may accrue to me if I try to do this kind of wicked thing) and more concerned with compassion, with sympathy for the misfortunes into which human beings often unwittingly plunge themselves. If the interests of the Greek dramatists could be described as primarily metaphysical, concerned with examining the relations between men and the gods, and the interests of the post-Renaissance theorists were essentially moral, it might be true to say that Corneille's real focus of interest is narrowing on the psychological. Consistent with his view is his approval of Aristotle's statement that the most powerful situations are offered when friend kills friend, so that commiseration is excited in the hearts of the audience.

A detailed consideration of the poet's handling of his material, bearing in mind the 'laws' of probability and necessity, forms the concluding section of this essay. The ancients took few liberties with history and kept their tragedies within a few families but the poet needs some scope for invention, so long as he maintains the general truth which is at the heart of all poetry and follows in his portrayal of character the common run of natural affections. Things may be presented as they have happened, in which case we are dealing with historical truth. Or they may be presented as it is said they have happened and that is to deal in fable, myth or legend. Or they may be presented in such manner as is likely or probable, so that 'vraisemblance' is maintained. Action may be accompanied by inseparable circumstances of time and place, so that a strict adherence to the unities becomes impossible. (Here he casts an envious eye on the novelist who has the whole earth at his command.) In such an action, the writer should strive for probability. Even if things did not happen or could not have happened in this way, they should be made to look as if they did. On the other hand there is the action which develops from a previous situation of necessity and there may be a conflict between the two actions when necessity – the logic of the situation – demands that an action occur but it is not possible for it to occur in the time available or at the supposed place. If such a conflict should arise (and the dramatist should try to avoid it arising) he will find that necessity, situational logic, will supervene over circumstances of time and place, leading to some loss in probability.

Actions in general fall into three categories. They follow history, in which case truth is evidently maintained; or they add to history, in which case the additions must maintain probability as to attendant circumstances of time and place and must follow the laws of logical sequence (i.e. necessity) from what has gone before; or they may fly in the face of history, falsify it, and this can only be justified by necessity. If something is said to happen which did not happen, the situation must be presented as if it were inevitable, bound by the law of logical consequence. Aristotle allows that a convincing impossibility is preferable to an unconvincing possibility. An action may demonstrate general probability without adhering to the particular facts of history. The action of *Nicomède* did not in fact happen but it is made acceptable by its treatment, which follows a logical sequence. The poet invokes necessity in order to achieve his purpose. After all, the end of the poet is to please in accordance with the rules of his art and in order to do so he may have to use some violence on the accepted order of things. Probability will sometimes have to be stretched to the limit and the safest practical guide for the writer is to be as vague as he can about time and place at the beginning of his play, then his audience will not feel bound and he will not require to ask their indulgence, for, and he quotes Horace: 'It is better not to need grace than to receive it'.

A more detailed consideration of the three unities provides the material for Corneille's third discourse. The unity of action is summed up in the case of comedy as unity of intrigue (obstacles are to be overcome) and for tragedy as unity of peril, to which the hero either succumbs or which he survives. A tragedy must have a beginning, a middle and an end but within this formal structure there will be minor actions related to the main action. Each act should close on a note of expectation as to what will happen in the next act but the audience does not need to know what each character is supposed to be doing between the acts. The action must form a sequential pattern and not be contingent. Corneille is as insistent on this as William Archer was to be two centuries later. Proper manipulation of the *liaison des scènes* though not essential at all times helps to establish the formal security of the play. Lengthy and detailed back narration should be avoided and the denouement of the play must maintain its own logic to a proper conclusion:[17]

> I find that two things are to be avoided in the denouement, the simple change of will and the use of the machine (*deus ex machina*). There is not much skill in finishing off a play in such a way that he who has been an obstacle to the plans of the principal actors for the duration of four acts leaves off in the fifth act without any obvious event compelling him so to do. The machine is not very skilfully used when it only serves to bring down a god who sorts everything out, at that point where the actors have no idea how to finish the play off.   (p. 368)

From the action he passes to the acts. Although five is the recognised number, the Greeks make no mention of this and the Spaniards and Italians occasionally have but three. He is not in favour of choric songs dividing up the acts. To pay attention to such singing is to strain the mind and not to relax. Not to pay attention is to encourage a scattering of concentration and a failure when the next act opens, to recall how the previous act had ended. Within the act there can be any number of scenes as long as the poet ensures that entrances and exits are adequately motivated. There is nothing in such bad taste as an actor leaving the stage simply because he has no more to say. This is not so important for entrances, and no explanation should be necessary as to why an actor is in a certain place at the opening of a play.

The subsequent comment on stage directions is interesting because it is one more pointer indicating how Corneille's theory of drama is reflecting a steady move towards naturalism which will culminate in the near-documentalist approach advocated by Sebastian Mercier in the following century. Corneille points out that Aristotle believes tragedy can be appreciated without actors or

[17] Corneille, *Œuvres.*

performance, i.e. solely from the text. In that case, texts should be provided generously with stage directions, something the ancients did not do, so the reader is often in the dark as to what is happening. Provision of stage directions, he adds, is also helpful for the company touring the provinces. A few stated directions will ensure that they avoid peculiar and embarrassing mistakes.

Corneille accepts the neo-classical interpretation of the time and place rules almost without demur although he recognises that holding the action of the play within twenty-four hours frequently drives the playwright close to infringement of the rule of probability, a matter which he has already considered in the second discourse. He cites Aeschylus in the *Agamemnon* and Euripides in *The Suppliants* as stretching credibility to the limit, much more so than he himself did in *Le Cid* or *Pompée*. Nonetheless, even without relying on Aristotle's authority, we must admit the reasonableness of the time limitation:

The dramatic poem is an imitation, or, to put it better, a portrait, of human action; and there is no question that portraits are better the more they resemble the original. The performance lasts two hours and would be a perfect representation if the action it covered last no more in reality. (p. 372)

So even if two hours be inadequate, let us at least stop at not much more than twenty-four. Beyond that, we will get nothing but a reduced picture of the action, an imperfect miniature. Unity of place, not mentioned by Aristotle or Horace he notes, is awarded a similar qualified concession. The ancients made things easier for themselves by having their kings speak in public places. That is not possible for us so let us expand our location 'to cover a town or least two or three places within the town walls'. Changes of scene must never take place within an act, and two places should not need different settings or individual names. This would be to thrust the scene change too obviously in front of the audience. Let us compromise on a generalised set which can stand for several places. Often, he admits, he has found it necessary to stretch the rule of place. Easy enough for the theorists to be rigorous but let them work on ten or a dozen plays 'and they'll maybe stretch the rules even more than I have done' once they have learned by experience how many good things would be lost through too much preciseness. And that, he concludes, is the best he can do in coming to contemporary terms with the ancient rules.

Like D'Aubignac, Corneille is concerned with isolating certain specific problems which confront the dramatist who would write creatively, but unlike D'Aubignac, he is able to take a wide embracing view of the whole theatrical landscape as it affected the writer in the middle years of the century. From the three discourses, there develops a consistent theory of drama which identifies the growing points in a changing theatre. Corneille's revised version of catharsis has moved well away from the position of the Italian critics. The exemplary function of the theatre, the need for tragedy to point a moral, these are no longer of first importance. Tragedy is impinging on the pathetic so that the dramatic experience is more concerned with pity than with fear. Pity is the tribute we pay in recognition of our closeness to the characters on the stage whose suffering might be ours, although our pity is spiced with admiration for the greatness of soul displayed before us, a greatness the like of which we members of the community will not aspire to. This new bearing along the psychological axis is paralleled by a clear statement about the nature of art. That kind of imitation which is in the nature of art, including painting and drama, to provide, is tending more and more to become qualitatively assessed in relation to its resemblance to the original. Mimesis is a version of lifelike portraiture, not because in Castelvetrian terms the rude multitude need resemblances spelled out to them in the simplest terms, but because it is the function of art to copy nature. The ideal conception of art which Sidney so well illustrated in his goldenbrazen metaphor is being replaced by a naturalistic conception which asks for a substitute world rather than an idealised world. Drama has still a long way to go before it becomes wholly naturalistic but Corneille in his role of critic is already providing the draft of a new programme.

René Rapin (1621–1687) being a stern Jesuit might be expected to take us back to the strong moral position of the counter-Reformationists and in his *Réflexions sur la Poétique d'Aristote* (Paris 1674)[18] he sees the theatre of his day dissolving into worthless frivolities. With the traditional neo-classical interpretation of catharsis he has no quarrel:

Of the various headings in the *Poetics*, that concerned with tragedy is the one which Aristotle has dealt with in most detail, and most methodically. He claims that tragedy offers a public lesson incomparably more instructive than anything that philosophy can provide, because it instructs the spirit through the senses and because it uses the passions to set the passions right, emotior itself being used to calm the excitement which the passions arouse in the heart. This scholar had recognised that these were two serious faults that had to be put right in men, pride and lack of compassion, and he found the remedy for these two faults in tragedy. Tragedy makes men humble in demonstrating to them how the great are brought low and it makes them sensitive, moving them to pity in putting in front of them on the stage the strange accidents of life and the unexpected degradations to which even the most important

[18] Translations are from this edition.

people are subject. But because man is by nature timid and sympathetic, he may fall into the other extremity of being either too fearful or too compassionate: too much timidity may weaken a man's spiritual fibre and too much compassion may militate against true justice. Tragedy is concerned with adjusting these two weaknesses. It ensures that we are not unacquainted with the nature of disgrace in seeing it so often engulf people of great moment and that we cease to worry about ordinary everyday accidents when we see them happen out of the blue to important persons. And since the end of tragedy is to teach men not to fear with too much weakness those ordinary downfalls and to control their fears, so also is it concerned with teaching them to confine their pity to those occasions when it is genuinely deserved. For it is unjust to be moved by the misfortunes of those who deserve to be miserable.

One can see Clytemnestra killed by her son Orestes (in Aeschylus) without any pity because she had cut the throat of her husband Agamemnon and one cannot see Hippolytus die through the plotting of Phedra, his stepmother, (in Euripides) without compassion, because he dies only for having been chaste and virtuous. This then seems to me, admirable: but his system has never been explained as it deserves by his interpreters, who have perhaps not been able to understand the mystery of it well enough in order to clarify it adequately.   (ch. XVII, pp. 181–2)

This reading of Aristotle is obviously close to that of Minturno and Scaliger. Given the straightforward proposition that the primary purpose of tragedy is to instruct, the moralistic interpretation of catharsis inevitably follows. Unlike Corneille, Rapin does not ask whether this in fact is what does happen; he is content that it should be assumed to happen. Tragedy, for Rapin, presents neither the ideal world of poetry nor the substitute world of naturalism made exciting through *grandeur*; it is simply a demonstration of human conduct from which lessons may be learned. The moralist pays some regard to the pleasurable aspect of drama if for no better reason than that stark sermonising by itself would neither fill the theatre nor meet with Aristotle's unqualified approval. If the mind is to be cured of vain fears, the cure must be through the emotions, through that agitation of the soul by the passions which will constitute a pleasure of the mind:

It is not enough that tragedy avails itself of all the most moving and most terrible avengers that history can provide, in order to excite in the heart those emotions that it lays claim to, for the purpose of curing the mind of those vain fears, which may trouble it, and of such foolish tenderness as may make it soft. So it is essential, says this philosopher, that every poet makes use of these great objects of fear and pity as the two most powerful springs which art possesses, so as to produce that pleasure which tragedy can give. And this pleasure which is properly a pleasure of the mind, consists in the agitation of the soul stimulated by the passions.   (ch. xviii, p. 182)

Here the argument takes a turn away from doctrinaire moralism to consider the response of the spectator as he watches a tragedy. He will fear, hope, rejoice with the characters on the stage. They are not mere *exempla*: they are fellow human beings with whom we will share an emotional experience and in the sharing we will know a special kind of pleasure, a delight, a reflective charm.

Tragedy becomes agreeable to the spectator:

...when he himself becomes sensible to all that is put before him, when he enters into all the different sentiments of the actors, when he becomes involved in their adventures, when he fears, when he hopes, when he sorrows and when he rejoices with them. That theatre is dead and boring which ceases to provide its audience with this kind of excitement of the soul. But since of all the passions pity and fear are those which make the greatest impression on the heart of man on account of his natural disposition to experience, on the one hand fear, on the other undue tenderness of heart, Aristotle has selected them out of all the others, to make a stronger impact on the spirit through those tender sentiments which they cause, when the heart allows itself to be touched by them. Indeed, when the soul is moved by these natural and human emotions, every single impression it feels becomes delightful. This disturbance pleases the soul and whatever emotion it feels possesses a kind of charm, which projects it into a pleasant and profound meditation and which makes it share, unconsciously as it were, all the interests which are the business of the theatre. Then it is that the heart gives itself over to all the objects which are put in front of it, that every image makes its impact, that it accepts the sentiments of all those who speak and that it becomes susceptible to all the passions which are shown it, because it is moved. And the whole of the pleasure that one is capable of getting from tragedy consists in this emotion. For the human spirit is pleased with those different situations which are caused by different objects and by the various passions that are represented. (ch. xviii, pp. 182–3)

He continues with an appreciative analysis of *Oedipus Rex*: 'Everything is terrible in this play and everything is moving'. But nowadays, alas, something has gone wrong with tragedy.

Modern tragedy works on different principles, possibly because the spirit of our nation could not maintain easily an action on the stage simply by rousing fear and pity. These are media which can only function adequately in the ambience of fine sentiments and superb rhetoric which we are not capable of providing quite in the Grecian manner. It may well be that our country, by nature addicted to gallantry, has been obliged perforce as a consequence of its character, to devise a new system of tragedy more suited to its temperament. (ch. xx, p. 186)

The democratic Greeks enjoyed seeing the humiliation of kings and the reversal of noble fortunes but the French seem to be more concerned with gallantry, the presentation of soft and tender sentiments. For this degradation he blames the ladies in the audience, who have 'promoted themselves arbiters and judges of these amusements'.

So we've become used to seeing heroes on the stage obsessed by a different kind of love from the love of glory, and thus have all the great figures of antiquity been reduced in stature when they go through our hands. So it is, perhaps, that the gallantry of our age has undertaken to make up for the poverty of its genius, being oftentimes unable to support the theme by the majesty of word or sentiment. However that may be, for I am not bold enough to come out against the general view, you untune the genuinely majestic note of tragedy if you get it mixed up with love which is always a light-hearted topic little suited to the seriousness which tragedy demands. Tragedies punctuated by scenes of gallantry completely fail to move the spirit in the manner of Sophoclean or Euripidean tragedy, for those tremendous scenes of fear and pity which these authors present struck home to the hearts of the audience. (ch. **xx**, pp. 186–7)

This is a shrewd comment in so far as it qualifies and places his previous remarks concerning that perturbation of the soul which is in itself a kind of delight. Comparing his present theatre with the Greek, he recognises a softening at the core which is detracting in his view from both the moral, and in a sense the psychological, rigour which he expects from true classical tragedy. He is regretting the loss of that *grandeur d'âme*, that sense of the mystery of living and that acquaintance with the fear one experiences in watching a man at the end of his tether, all of which Rapin finds satisfyingly and completely in Greek Tragedy:

Whatever has some weight and seriousness on the stage, even if pleasing for the moment, is liable to become stale afterwards, and whatever is not allied to the fine sentiments and tremendous roles of tragedy will not last for long. The ancients, who were aware of this, did not introduce gallantry and love except in their comedies. For it is the nature of love to detract from that heroic tone which is essential to tragedy. Nothing seems to me more senseless than being amused by amorous badinage and frivolity when one can be moved to wonder by the marvels of fine sentiments and splendid scenes. But I have hardly sufficient standing on my own account to oppose such a well-established habit. I must be content by expressing my doubts.   (ch. xx, p. 187)

As a moralist, Rapin demands of tragedy that it be doctrinal. As a philosopher and a sensitive reader, he is aware of the inexplicable power, the moving spirit, that lies behind a dramatic presentation of the tragic dilemma. The pleasure in tragedy, he says, is emotional, but he feels that the drama of his own day no longer finds its source in the depths of human passion. Fear and pity are basic emotions and when they are not roused in full measure, the theatre is failing to confront man with a true picture of his condition. Such a picture, in Rapin's view, is not complete if it confines itself to a representation, however painstakingly detailed, of man's relation to woman. He is not prepared to admit the tragedy of sentimental love into the first rank of dramatic literature.

André Dacier (1651–1722) provides a concluding chapter to French seventeenth-century criticism by publishing in 1692 his *Poetics of Aristotle with Critical Commentary.*[19] A mild-mannered scholar, steeped in the classics, claiming his position as an ancient in the quarrel between the ancients and the moderns, he nevertheless indicates in his criticism a move towards eighteenth-century sentimentalism. Like Rapin he is reluctantly aware that the time for the old drama is past and he is far

[19] *La Poétique d'Aristote avec des remarques critiques.* Translations are from this edition.

from anxious to welcome the new. The rules, he states in his preface, are not incompatible with pleasure. At the same time we must remember that drama is an art with a purpose and its rules encourage it to seek the good and avoid the bad. These rules, although enunciated by Aristotle, are not a body of law laid down by him. They are based on reason, on experience and so are as valid today as they were in ancient Greece. There is plenty of bad drama which entertains the audience 'by the complication and denouement of an empty intrigue aiming to stimulate and satisfy curiosity and inflaming the passions instead of satisfying or subduing them', but this is not art since it does not aim at any good. The good and the beautiful is that which is in harmony with nature and this harmony can be recognised both by feeling and by reason. In tragedy, an ordered mode of providing pleasure and instruction, we learn to purify and curb our passions. The ambitious man learns to limit his ambition, the impious to fear God and so on. Tragedy is in short a moral allegory; its aim is instruction through entertainment. The chorus should be brought back for the purpose of underlining the moral.

There follows in this preface to the commentary the usual defensive remarks aimed at proving to the reader that this is the best work of its kind ever to appear:

The Italian Castelvetro has a deal of understanding and knowledge, if one can take the product of a vivid imagination and call it understanding or give the name of knowledge to a fine lecture. Think of all the qualities of a good commentator, turn them inside out and you've got a true picture of Castelvetro. He understands neither theatre, passions nor characters, neither the reasoning nor the method of Aristotle and he is more concerned with contradicting him than explaining him. He is so engrossed with the writers of his own country that he disables himself from being a sound critic... *La Pratique du*

*Théâtre* by l'Abbé D'Aubignac is infinitely better but it is less an explanation of Aristotle than a follow-up, a supplement, the worth of which (or lack of it) can only be judged in the light of a thorough acquaintance with the rules. *Le Traité du Poème Epique* by Le Bossu is better than anything the moderns have done in this direction... (Preface).

Corneille has next to be challenged because he claimed that commentators should have experience of the theatre, a qualification to which obviously Dacier did not aspire:

It would appear that those who have never written poems ought not to undertake the explanation of the rules of poetry. The principle is sound but the consequence is not so because before coming to this conclusion, it is necessary to examine where the art of poetry properly belongs and how it is produced. Poetry is not spun out of itself; it is philosophy which has given it birth, and consequently it is the function of philosophy to establish and to explain the rules. This is sufficiently obvious in so far as Aristotle did not lay down his rules in the person of a poet but in the person of a philosopher, and if he speaks as a philosopher, why should we not explain his rules in terms of philosophy? Since it is unnecessary to have written plays in order to establish rules for this kind of writing, it is equally unnecessary for him who would explain the rules to be a dramatist. (Preface)

Having made his point, disclaimed any desire for fame, and undertaken to speak freely and spare nothing or no one, he settles down to a detailed consideration of *The Poetics* chapter by chapter. His comments on imitation, the nature of comedy and the unity of time throw no new light on these topics. His gloss on Aristotle's sixth chapter introducing the idea of catharsis begins with a refutation of Corneille's view that 'purging' is a good idea which does not work in practice; nor, says Dacier, are those interpreters right who say this passage is simply an answer to Plato's attack on the poets. It is wrong to think of the purging process as a rooting out of the passions, because these are the soul's strength. Purging really means to get rid of an excess, so acquaintance with tragedy in the theatre becomes a kind of moral athletics, a spiritual toning up; the excess fats of passion are disposed of. Vicarious acquaintance with misfortune prepares us for the real thing. People like ourselves are plunged into misfortune through involuntary mistakes and we are conscious of our closeness to their situation. In company with Rapin he agrees that we learn not to be too afraid or too grief-stricken when calamity strikes us:

Here then is the first effect of Tragedy, that it purges fear and pity by working through these passions. Thus it gives no little profit to men for it prepares them to endure with courage the most heart-breaking mishaps and puts the most miserable of men in the way of thinking themselves fortunate when they compare their own miseries with those depicted in tragedy. Whatever state a man may be in, when he sees an Oedipus, a Philoctetes, an Orestes, he cannot but think his miseries light compared with theirs. But tragedy doesn't rest there. In purging fear and pity, it purges at the same time all the other passions which might throw us into the same state of misery, for in exposing the faults which bring pain and suffering to these miserable men, tragedy teaches us to be on our guard against falling into similar dire straits and to purge and moderate that passion which has brought about their downfall. For example, anyone seeing Sophocles' *Oedipus* will learn to correct his own rashness and blind curiosity, for these rather than crime are the causes of his misfortunes. (ch. VI, p. 82)

In common with other critics of his time, Dacier is concerned about Aristotle's statement that you can have tragedy without character but not without action. Corneille's reading is wrong. What Aristotle means is that a tragedy without character is one in which the characters speak in such a way that they do not reveal their feelings and one couldn't tell from their speech what decision they will take next. In tragedy, plot is more important; in comedy character is more essential than theme. His consideration of the ninth chapter of the *Poetics* reaches the well-established conclusion that the poet, having access to universals, being able to make generalised statements – not what did happen but what might or could happen – is more worthy of a hearing than the historian who is bound by facts, is never aware of primary causes, is confined to recital as compared with visible action, and works alone in his field, unlike the dramatist who, allying himself with the theologian and the natural philosopher, in addition summons the passions to underline his case.

The view that tragedy is about kings and princes is denied in Dacier's treatment of Aristotle's thirteenth chapter. Granted, he says, that tragedy must arouse fear and pity. The misfortunes of a very wicked man arouse neither. Fear and pity are passions which are aroused by the misfortunes of *people like ourselves*. To see virtue suffering unjustifiably is to invite despair. Corneille objected to this because martyrs – including his Polyeucte – were therefore banished from the theatre. Furthermore, if tragedy is to involve pity, fear and pleasure, the wicked must not profit, nor is it worthwhile to show the wicked being punished. Is it indeed worthwhile to show the misfortunes of kings and princes, men so unlike ourselves? Corneille uses an *a fortiori* argument – if we see kings and princes, so far above us, so stricken, surely the lesson is all the stronger. But this is wrong. There is no need to draw a distinction between kings and princes and all men in general. This was not Aristotle's intention:

The true answer can be taken straight from Aristotle's writing. He has already demonstrated that the subject of Tragedy is first and foremost a universal fable, which concerns all men in general. It is not Oedipus or Atreus or Thyestes but an ordinary man to whom one gives whatever name one likes. But to add to the grandeur and vraisemblance of his action, the Poet gives him an illustrious name which will be recognised. Yet however much the fable may appear to be about particular people, through such an application of names, it does not change its fundamental nature but continues to be concerned with the general. The action concerns an ordinary man even though he be called a Prince or a King. So Aristotle was right to call those Princes and Kings our 'semblables'; for the poet has no intention of imitating the actions of Kings, but the actions of men; we are the people he is representing. (p. 189)

Men in a lowly position, he goes on, often experience extraordinary and quite tragic adventures but as tragic figures they would fail because they are not impressive enough. The action of tragedy must be important and great if it is to be acceptable and convincing, but the context in which the action takes place must bear a sufficiently close resemblance to the world of the ordinary man so that the latter will recognise that the same laws prevail in his world as in that of the tragic hero. Dacier's treatment of *hamartia* continues this line of thought. There are three kinds of 'fault':

(1) a human fault or failing;
(2) an unwilled mistake, the consequence of some overmastering passion; or
(3) a mistake deriving out of a divine or supernatural order.

The crime of Oedipus is of the first kind and also partially rests on the second; that of Thyestes is of the second and those of Orestes and Alcmæon of the third kind. Corneille seems to think Oedipus is not guilty of any crime because he kills his father in ignorance. Corneille has misunderstood the character of Oedipus as represented by Sophocles:

As to the fault of Oedipus, it is the fault of a man who, carried away by anger at a coachman's insolence, kills four men two days after the oracle has warned him that he would kill his own father...This one action would adequately mark out his character but Sophocles has given him in all respects attributes in keeping with his action, in perfect conformity with Aristotle's rules, so that one sees continually a man who is neither wholly good nor wholly wicked and who demonstrates a mingling of virtues and vices. His vices are pride, violence, unbridled passion, rashness and imprudence. It is not in fact his incest or his parricide which brings about his downfall. Such punishment would have been in some way unjust, since these crimes were entirely involuntary and he committed them in ignorance. He meets with these dreadful calamaties, solely as a result of his curiosity, his rashness and his resort to physical violence...These are the vices Sophocles wants to correct in us.    (p. 192)

Dacier seems here to be pointing to a new kind of sensibility, that there is justice in the universe and if man wills himself to adhere to the moral law, he will benefit from that justice. Good will come out of good and evil will come from wickedness. Essentially man is master of his fate. So it is in the case of Thyestes, who allowed wrath to rule him. Let us take note that anger and the unbridled desire for vengeance lead to injustice. The idea of 'poetical justice' (a phrase coined by Rymer long before Dacier's work was published) suits the temper of the new age. Knowledge of this justice demands that if man seems to be deserted by it, he must find an adequate reason and this he finds within himself, in his failure to control his passions, in the weakness of his own character. There is of course sadness in tragedy, a condition inseparable from that kind of tragic action which is thrust upon us, but even so, some kind of redeemable error lies behind the action. We may shed a sympathetic tear for the victim who seems to be singled out for sacrifice against his will, but we can at the same time establish for ourselves that error is present, even although, as in the case of Oedipus the hero's sufferings appear to be more terrible than his crime. In comedy, on the other hand, disorder is put right and events are reconciled. Dacier feels that some French comedies err on the side of punishing the hero overmuch: 'I never come away from the *The Misanthrope* for example without feeling sorry for Alceste – this displeases me'.

Those seventeenth-century French critics whose principal works on dramatic theory have been briefly examined above were engaged on a similar quest which had the twofold aim of justifying the theatre as a valuable social activity and summarising – with the *Poetics* as a basic primer – those conditions of composition which would provoke predictable responses in the theatre. Behind most of the arguments there lurks the assumption that prescriptive rules may be generated from some kind of objective truth and can have their validity checked not only by an appeal to the ancients but to reason as well, so that eventually the rule of Aristotle may be found to coincide with the rule of nature. By far the most subtle of these critics is Corneille. Unlike Chapelain, he appreciated and confronted the dilemma set up when the rule of probability, centring on time and place, clashed with the rule of necessity stemming from the demands of a logically sequential action. He was equally concerned about the validity of current interpretations of catharsis and came out against the fashionable trend of thought (fashionable, that is, in the view of the theorists if not so often maintained by the practitioners) by declaring that the central interest in tragedy was psychological, stemming from pity, from fellow feeling for the victim, rather than moral. This is a distinct move away from D'Aubignac whose concern for moral teaching, for verisimilitude (achieved by a strict logic of action, time and place) and for tight structure perhaps places him as the last of the Scaligerian formalists. His contribution to theory is retrospective in the sense of collecting up all that has gone before, rather than developmental in the Corneillian sense.

Rapin, after a deal of discursive manoeuvring, would seem eventually to take up a position among the moderns. While ostensibly disagreeing with Corneille on the doctrinal purpose and moral effect of tragedy, which he feels is clearly stated by Aristotle, Rapin pursues his argument to the point of admitting that tragedy is concerned with the heart 'giving itself over', becoming 'susceptible to all the passions which are shown to it' and that 'the whole of the pleasure that one is capable of getting from tragedy consists in this emotion'. The language is if anything stronger than that used by Corneille and reveals a genuine sympathy with the new 'psychological' critics rather than with the old moral school. The pleasure of tragedy is no longer the pleasure of learning by watching an imitation but rather the pleasure of feeling with the characters on the stage. He is at the same time chary of too much trivial sentiment which he thinks is the regrettable end-product of the theatre's obsession with sexual love, gallantry, and at the lowest level, badinage and frivolity.

Dacier, who, even more than Rapin, is probably the most frequently quoted French critic in later English dramatic criticism, goes over the catharsis argument in terms which occasionally strike a modern note. Purging gets rid of an excess of passion, he says, not only the passions of pity and fear but all passions, hate, envy and so on, which might add to our misery. One seems to have heard something like this in present-day discussions about 'violence' on the stage and screen, that the display of violence and the vicarious joining-in reduces or 'sublimates' the aggressive tendency of the spectator. So far however no one seems to have proved satisfactorily that displays of mimetic violence do not in fact encourage real violence.

Dacier's insistence that tragedy should reflect a just universe would have had only qualified approval, if any at all, from Scaliger. As has been shown, the early neo-classical critics dictate a moral approach which presupposes the depravity of man and his dependence on the mercy of God. Tragedy plays its part in reinforcing the warning: 'The whole atmosphere is one of uncertainty, fear, threats, exile and death'. Now, Dacier would have tragedy provide a vision of an improvable world. If Oedipus had been less bad-tempered at the cross-roads, less curious about his destiny, less convinced that he could solve all riddles including his own, he could have avoided his tragic fate. Not only is this a simplistic moral view, but by ignoring the attributes of wonder, magnificence, *grandeur*, or at best giving them only a cursory mention, Dacier has reduced tragedy to something of less consequence than either Corneille or Rapin would have accepted. By domesticating Oedipus, he is already looking ahead to the new conception of drama as being concerned with people like ourselves, which will be developed by Diderot and Mercier in the next century.

# 4

## The English scene – Restoration and early eighteenth-century criticism

The opinions of those few seventeenth-century French critics outlined in the previous chapter may serve as an introduction to the dramatic criticism of John Dryden (1631–1700) and his successors in the English tradition. A collection of recent commentaries on Dryden as a critic takes us into a busy area of scholarship where, if we are passers-by rather than sojourners, we may feel our position tenuous. Louis I. Bredvold started a long debate in 1934 with *The Intellectual Milieu of John Dryden*[1] but his proposition that Dryden was sceptical (in the full technical sense of the term, i.e. a Pyrrhonist) and fideistic would seem to have been refuted by both Harth (*Contexts of Dryden's Thought*) and Hume (*Dryden's Criticism*). Harth concludes his opening chapter with what might be described as a moderate view: 'Unquestionably scepticism is an important part of Dryden's characteristic thought. But it is a very different matter from the Pyrrhonism with which it has been so long identified. Indeed, it is in certain respects the very opposite. Far from being a sign of Dryden's anti-rationalism, his scepticism is a confident affirmation of the powers of

[1] Republished in Ann Arbor Paperbacks, 1966. Other essential reading would include: *The Place of Rules in Dryden's Criticism* by Hoyt Trowbridge, first pub. in *Modern Philology* vol. 44 (1946) but more easily obtainable in *Essential Articles for the Study of John Dryden*, ed. Swedenborg; *Dryden's Apparent Scepticism in 'Religio Laici'* by Elias J. Chiasson, first pub. in *The Harvard Theological Review* vol. LIV (1961) reprinted in *Dryden's Mind and Art*, ed. King; *Contexts of Dryden's Thought* by P. Harth; *Dryden's Criticism* by R. D. Hume.

human reason. When unexamined opinion is accepted as a substitute for honest investigation, Dryden believed, reason is betrayed and truth made captive.'

As a preliminary to fitting Dryden into our study of dramatic theory in this period, we would hazard four propositions: (1) that Dryden held that truth was tentative and provisional until it had been tested by doubt, although eventually through reason truth would declare itself; (2) that in common with his peers he looked on the making of poetry, including drama, as a skill which could be the better performed if some basic rules were adopted; (3) that he was much more strongly influenced by French theories (particularly those of Corneille, and Rapin through Rymer) than he himself would be prepared to admit; (4) that he looked on poetry as a heightened reflection of nature (not a literal representation) and certainly not as a 'branch of knowledge' in the Johnsonian sense as, for instance, Daiches would have it.[2]

The method of *An Essay of Dramatic Poesy* (1668) suited Dryden's speculative approach to the problems of literary craftsmanship as he saw them. Couched in the form of a debate between four speakers, the *Essay* is probably more profitably read as the reflections of one man examining varying and sometimes contradictory propositions so that he may in the long run 'by indirections find directions out'. His definition of a play, closer to Donatus and Scaliger than to Aristotle, is sufficiently general to allow scope for his problematical method of enquiry. Using the voice of Crites, he outlines the case for ancient drama, making the provocative point – later considered in more detail by nineteenth-century critics and maintained by T. S. Eliot – that 'every age has a kind of universal genius which inclines those that live in it to

[2] *Critical Approaches to Literature*, D. Daiches, ch. 4.

some particular studies'. Dramatic poetry in fifth-century Greece was 'pushed on by many hands' but in seventeenth-century Europe, philosophy, not poetry, dominates the interests of men. When he comes to the unities, Crites relies on Corneille to state his case. Time should be restricted as nearly as possible to twenty-four hours and place should not move out of the same town or city. Eugenius brings the argument up to date by claiming that we follow not the ancients, but nature and by so doing have improved on the old poetry, particularly in adopting the rule that vice must be punished and virtue rewarded.

Corneille is again the source of Lisideius' pro-French arguments in favour of tight structure, rigorous unity of action and the grounding of tragedies on a known history. The French avoid the visual presentation of cruelty, the peril of unbelief through offering an impossible action, the 'tumult' associated with attempts to bring whole armies on the stage and the disproportionate extension of the time bracket. Dryden, through Lisideius, is admitting a qualified partiality for tight structure and formal pattern, a bare sinewy play with few characters and conditions which encourage 'verisimility'. Having said this, he immediately inverts the argument by claiming through Neander that the French beauties are the 'beauties of a statue'. There is no reason why tragedy and comedy should not come together in the same play. French verses are cold and declamations unnatural, and as for tumults, why should we not persuade ourselves that the blows are given in good earnest, just as we accept that actors are kings and princes. Even Corneille himself admits that writers are limited and constrained by rules, whereas English plots are fuller of variety and our drama has on the whole a more masculine fancy and greater spirit. To illustrate his point, Neander chooses to give a criticism of Jonson's *The Silent Woman* wherein he finds qualities which seem to him to represent the best of both the French and the English comic theatre. The unities are rigorously adhered to, as is continuity of scene but variety is added in the English manner through the introduction of 'by-walks and under-plots as diversions to the main design' though they are still naturally joined with it. So nine or ten different characters are all used to the conducting of the main design: unity is maintained in the midst of diversity. The portrayal of Morose is defended as being probable since it is not unusual to find people of delicate hearing to whom all sharp sounds are unpleasant, and being an old man he is peevish and jealous of his authority in his own house.

The *Essay* concludes with a discussion on the relative virtues of blank verse or rhymed couplets as the proper medium for stage dialogue. Neander replies to Crites who has asked why it has been assumed during their talk that rhyme is proper for the stage, and has gone on to make the case for blank verse:[3]

But I come now to the inference of your first argument. You said that the dialogue of plays is presented as the effect of sudden thought, but no man speaks suddenly, or extempore, in rhyme; and you inferred from thence, that rhyme, which you acknowledge to be proper to epic poesy, cannot equally be proper to dramatic, unless we could suppose all men born so much more than poets, that verses should be made in them, not by them.

It has been formerly urged by you, confessed by me, that since no man spoke any kind of verse extempore, that which is nearest to nature was to be preferred. I answer you, therefore, by distinguishing betwixt what is nearest to the nature of comedy, which is the imitation of common persons and ordinary speaking, and what is nearest the nature of a serious

[3] Quotations from John Dryden, *Dramatic Essays.*

play; this last is indeed the representation of nature, but 'tis nature wrought up to a higher pitch. The plot, the characters, the wit, the passions, the descriptions, are all exalted above the level of common converse, as high as the imagination of the poet can carry them, with proportion to verisimility. Tragedy, we know, is wont to image to us the minds and fortunes of noble persons, and to portray these exactly; heroic rhyme is nearest nature, as being the noblest kind of modern verse.   (*Essay of Dramatic Poesy*, p. 54)

This argument is often treated as if it were solely concerned with rhetoric, i.e. there are two ways of saying the same thing, one in blank verse, the other in rhyme. On this level Neander makes the sound point – and again we recall the words of Eliot about 'overcoming' Shakespeare – that it will be better 'either not to write at all, or to attempt some other way' since blank verse has been pre-empted by Ben Jonson, Fletcher and Shakespeare. But the line of attack changes significantly when we come to the paragraphs quoted above. The achievement of a valid mimetic form is now the target. Does rhyme or blank verse bring us closer to that kind of mimesis which we look for in poetry of the highest order? At this stage in his thinking, and Dryden is by no means consistent, he argues that rhyme is essential in serious plays, not comedies, because as a form of rhetoric it provides a representation of nature 'wrought up to a higher pitch'. Everything must be exalted above the level of common converse 'with proportion to verisimility'. This is the crux of the matter, that the representation must be acceptable, probable, but not literal. Poetry is not a direct imitation of life. Nobility, and exaltation of the normal, is part of the stuff of serious poetry. No one argues that the author's utterances are spontaneous any more than the writing of the epic poet. Verse is not the effect of sudden thought but sudden thought may be represented in verse. This debate tends to be discarded by modern critics as totally obsolete and yet it is at the heart of any discussion about the true nature of dramatic dialogue. The question is not one of rhymed or un-rhymed verse – which superficially is what it looks like – but much more important, how close is the relationship we want to establish between the way in which people use words on the stage and off the stage? How far can the dramatic form, involving the visual presentation of living people, be conventionalised, removed from the 'creatural' world[4] – to use Auerbach's word – without totally severing the relationship between events on the stage and events in 'real life'. People going about their ordinary business do not speak in blank verse nor do they speak in rhymed couplets, so, in our naturalistic fictional world of contemporary drama and film we make them speak the prose of the market square, but this was too simple a solution for Dryden and his contemporaries or, more precisely, it is a solution which they would have considered irrelevant because it ignored the basic premise on which they built their theory of poetry, namely, that poetry is concerned with nature 'wrought up to a higher pitch'.

No sooner had *An Essay of Dramatic Poesy* appeared than Sir Robert Howard, Dryden's brother-in-law, who had originally started the debate by advocating blank verse in his *Preface to Four New Plays* (1665) returned to the attack in a *Preface to 'The Duke of Lerma'*:[5]

In the next place, I must ingeniously confess that the manner of plays which now are in most esteem is beyond my pow'r to perform; nor do I condemn in the least any thing of what

---

[4] *Mimesis*, E. Auerbach, p. 387.
[5] Quotations from *Critical Essays of the Seventeenth Century*, ed. Spingarn.

Nature soever that pleases, since nothing could appear to me a ruder folly than to censure the satisfaction of others; I rather blame the unnecessary understanding of some that have labour'd to give strict rules to things that are not Mathematical, and with such eagerness pursuing their own seeming reasons that at last we are to apprehend such Argumentative Poets will grow as strict as 'Sancho Panco's' Doctor was to our very Appetites; for in the difference of Tragedy and Comedy, and of Fars itself, there can be no determination but by the Taste; nor in the manner of their Composure; and who ever wou'd endeavour to like or dislike by the Rules of others, he will be as unsuccessful as if he should try to be perswaded into a power of believing, not what he must, but what others direct him to believe.

But I confess, 't is not necessary for Poets to study strict Reason, since they are so us'd to a greater Latitude than is allowed by that severe Inquisition, that they must infringe their own Jurisdiction to profess themselves oblig'd to argue well. I will not therefore pretend to say why I writ this Play, some Scenes in blank Verse, others in Rhime; since I have no better a reason to give than Chance, which waited upon my present Fancy, and I expect no better a reason from any ingenious person than his Fancy for which he best relishes.   (vol. ii, pp. 106–7)

Here, in a form of statement which would hardly measure up to Dryden's lofty standards of refinement, Howard rejects Aristotle, rules, and reason, in favour of 'taste', an element in literary evaluation which is to gain significance as the eighteenth century approaches and one with which Dryden would have no truck whatsoever. Poets, says Howard, have no need to study reason since they are answerable only to themselves and if they are inclined to use both blank verse and rhyme in the same play, that is their affair. There is no hierarchy, such as Dryden at this stage would maintain, whereby rhyme is superior to blank verse in being the proper mode for serious poetry. Howard now shifts his attack on pre-scribed verse forms to the traditional rules:

First, we are told the Plot should not be so ridiculously contriv'd as to crowd two several Countries into one stage; secondly, to cramp the Accidents of many years or dayes into the representation of two houres and a halfe: And Lastly, a conclusion drawn, that the only remaining dispute is concerning time, whether it should be contain'd in twelve or four and twenty hours, and the place to be limited to the spot of ground, either in Town or City, where the Play is suppos'd to begin: And this is call'd neerest to Nature; For that is concluded most natural which is most probable and neerest to that which it presents.

I am so well pleas'd with any ingenious offers, as all these are, that I should not examine this strictly, did not the confidence of others force me to it, there being not any thing more unreasonable to my Judgement than the attempt to infringe the Liberty of Opinion by Rules so little demonstrative.

To shew therefore upon what ill grounds they dictate Lawes for 'Dramatick Poesie', I shall endeavour to make it evident that there's no such thing as what they all pretend; for if strictly and duely weighed, 'tis as impossible for one stage to present two Houses or two Roomes truely as two Countreys or Kingdomes, and as impossible that five houres, or four and twenty houres should be two houres and a halfe as that a thousand houres or yeares should be less than what they are, or the gretest part of time to be comprehended in the less; for all being impossible, they are none of them nearest the truth or nature of what they present, for impossibilities are all equal, and admit no degrees.   (vol. II, pp. 108–9)

Dryden, in the *Defence of An Essay of Dramatic Poesy* (1668) quickly exposed the weaknesses in this argument. First, however, he had to answer Howard's comments on verse, which he does with a slight readjustment of his previous argument. Naturalness, he suggests, is not an issue, but pleasure is important and if good verse gives more

pleasure than prose, then verse justifies itself. Furthermore, and here he returns to a basic principle:[6]

T'is true that to imitate well is a poet's work: but to affect the
soul, and excite the passions, and above all to move admiration
which is the delight of serious plays, a bare imitation will not
serve. The converse, therefore, which a poet is to imitate, must
be heightened with all the arts and ornaments of poesy, and
must be such, as strictly considered, could never be supposed
spoken by any without premeditation.   (p. 62)

Prose in fact cannot be used in serious plays because:

it is too near the nature of converse: there may be too great
a likeness; as the most skilful painters affirm, that there may
be too near a resemblance in a picture; to take every lineament
and feature, is not to make an excellent piece, but to take so
much only as will make a beautiful resemblance of the whole;
and, with an ingenious flattery of nature, to heighten the
beauties of some parts, and hide the deformities of the rest.
(pp. 62–3)

As Dryden reflects on the nature of dramatic illusion,
the developing subtlety of the discussion on mimesis
becomes obvious. Imitation must embrace the 'flattery
of nature' so that even if the original be vile, 'the copy
is of price'. The poet's concern is not to transcribe nature
literally, but to give delight through his contrived presentation. The choice of a suitable verse form becomes
a matter of aesthetics as well as a technical problem
related to the achievement of verisimility. Taste, 'the
liking or disliking of the people' provides no criterion
because the people are just as likely to be pleased by bad
plays as by good ones. Poets must follow reason in so far
as they are bound by moral truth, so a bad argument
reflects a bad workman. As to the unities, if nature is to

[6] Dryden, *Dramatic Essays.*

be imitated, and that would seem to be the end of poetry, there must be right ways and wrong ways of carrying out the imitation. Everyone knows that when he is in a theatre, the real place is the theatre, but within the theatre there is an imaginary place, a fiction, for the evocation of which the poet relies on his words striking the imagination of his audience. This imagination has certain limits: its readiness to respond to given stimuli is governed by reason, so it is more likely to accept the fictional existence of two places which are nearer than two places which are further apart:[7]

Imagination in a man or reasonable creature is supposed to participate of reason; and when that governs, as it does in the belief of fiction, reason is not destroyed, but misled or blinded: that can prescribe to the reason, during the time of the representation, somewhat like a weak belief of what it sees and hears; and reason suffers itself to be so hoodwinked, that it may better enjoy the pleasures of the fiction: but it is never so wholly made a captive, as to be drawn headlong into a persuasion of those things which are most remote from probability: 'tis in that case a free-born subject, not a slave; it will contribute willingly its assent, as far as it sees convenient, but will not be forced. Now there is a greater vicinity in nature betwixt two rooms than betwixt two houses, betwixt two houses than betwixt two cities, and so of the rest; Reason therefore can sooner be led by Imagination to step from one room into another, than to walk to two distant houses, and yet rather to go thither, than to fly like a witch through the air and be hurried from one region to another. Fancy and Reason go hand in hand; the first cannot leave the last behind; and though Fancy, when it sees the wide gulf, would venture over as the nimbler, yet it is withheld by Reason, which will refuse to take the leap, when the distance over it appears too large. If Ben Jonson himself will remove the scene from Rome into Tuscany

[7] Dryden, *Dramatic Essays.*

in the same act, and from thence return to Rome, in the scene which immediately follows, reason will consider there is no proportionable allowance of time to perform the journey, and therefore will choose to stay at home. So, then, the less change of place there is, the less time is taken up in transporting the persons of the drama, with analogy to reason; and in that analogy, or resemblance of fiction to truth, consists the excellency of the play.

For what else concerns the unity of place, I have already given my opinion of it in my *Essay* – that there is a latitude to be allowed to it, – as several places in the same town or city, or places adjacent to each other in the same country, which may all be comprehended under the larger denomination of one place; yet with this restriction, that the nearer and fewer those imaginary places are, the greater resemblance they will have to truth: and reason, which cannot make them one, will be more easily led to suppose them so.

What has been said of the unity of place, may easily be applied to that of time: I grant it to be impossible that the greater part of time should be comprehended in the less, that twenty-four hours should be crowded into three: but there is no necessity of that supposition. For as 'Place', so 'Time' relating to a play, is either imaginary or real: the real is comprehended in those three hours, more or less, in the space of which the play is represented; the imaginary is that which is supposed to be taken up in the representation, as twenty-four hours more or less.   (pp. 72–3)

The originality of this statement lies in the proposition that Imagination and Reason are allies, not prisoner and gaoler. Reason may be 'hoodwinked' by the Imagination, the better to enjoy a delightful fiction. But just as Imagination should not be dominated by Reason, so Reason cannot be at the beck and call of Imagination. There is a happy point of conciliation, and this the dramatist must find by so structuring his scenes that any necessary movement between them is acceptable and structuring his time scale so that an absurd stretch of time is avoided. Dryden takes pains to point out that Corneille came to a similar conclusion. The rules are founded on reason but where they throw up insuperable aesthetic problems, i.e. if the consequence is the banishment of certain beauties from the stage, it is reasonable to temper their severity. Aristotle, if he mistakes not, is of the same opinion, 'that there are degrees in impossibilities' and the poet will refrain from presenting the absolutely impossible. While occasionally inconsistent on technical details – most notably in his treatment of blank and rhymed verse – Dryden is quite clear on the basic principles of his craft, one of which is that the rules as laid down by the ancients and revised by the French can be supported by reason and are, by and large, a good starting point for the poet.

It has been fashionable to argue that in his *Observations on Rymer's 'Remarks on the Tragedies of The Last Age'*, Dryden shows considerably less deference to the neo-classical tradition, but a close examination of the terms and tone of the *Observations* hardly bears this out. In the *Observations*, Dryden, engaged in his favourite pastime of talking to himself and writing down the ensuing dialogue, finds himself in a familiar dilemma, having to reconcile his respect for the ancients with his conviction that the English surpass them. Rymer is under no such obligation since he is prepared to condemn English drama almost totally and with equal vigour vindicate the ancients. Dryden's case for the moderns introduces few novelties, if any. English plots are more adorned with episodes than the Greek and therefore more diverting; Shakespeare and Fletcher present more, and more various, characters, but Greek characters are more adapted to the rousing of pity and terror. On the other hand, are pity and terror the prime, or at least, the only, ends of tragedy? It will be recalled that Corneille asked the same question:[8]

'Tis not enough that Aristotle has said so, for Aristotle drew his models of tragedy from Sophocles and Euripides; and if he had seen ours, might have changed his mind. And chiefly we have to say (what I hinted on pity and terror in the last paragraph save one) that the punishment of vice and reward of virtue are the most adequate ends of tragedy, because most conducing to good example of life. Now pity is not so easily raised for a criminal, and the ancient tragedy always represents its chief person such, as it is for an innocent man; and the suffering of innocence and punishment of the offender is of the nature of English tragedy; contrarily, in the Greek, innocence is unhappy often, and the offender escapes. Then we are not touched with the sufferings of any sort of men so much as of lovers; and this was almost unknown to the ancients; so that they neither administered poetical justice, of which Mr. Rymer boasts, so well as we; neither knew they the best common-place of pity, which is love.   (vol. I, pp. 474–5)

In his mental dialogue with Rymer, Dryden argues we have done better than the Greeks because we have invented the idea of poetical justice, whereby, even if the innocent suffer, the wicked shall certainly be punished. Since 'the great end of the poem is to instruct', this end is achieved through the poet demonstrating that virtue is to be praised and vice to be discouraged:[9]

To return to the beginning of this enquiry; consider if pity and terror be enough for tragedy to move: and I believe, upon a true definition of tragedy, it will be found that its work extends farther, and that it is to reform manners, by a delightful representation of human life in great persons, by way of dialogue. If this be true, then not only pity and terror are to be moved as the only means to bring us to virtue, but generally love

[8] Quotations from Samuel Johnson, *Lives of the English Poets.*
[9] Johnson, *Lives.*

to virtue and hatred to vice; by shewing the rewards of one and punishments of the other; at least by rendering virtue always amiable, tho' it be shewn unfortunate; and vice detestable, though it be shewn triumphant. (vol. I, pp. 476–7)

This is surely neo-classicism pure and undiluted, regardless of the fact that Aristotle would have denied the major premise that the 'great end of the poem is to instruct'. The influence of Rapin is apparent in the extension of the operative passions from pity and fear to include joy, anger and love. Such an extension of the emotional range of tragedy will help to generate that kind of pleasure which leads to instruction. What pleased a judicious Athenian audience will not necessarily please an English one, so Shakespeare and Fletcher wrote for the genius of the age and nation in which they lived, despite the 'wittily aggravated' faults which Rymer claimed to find in their designs.

Some time after writing the *Observations*, which were mere marginal comments not, presumably, intended for publication, Dryden completed an adaptation of Shakespeare's *Troilus and Cressida* (1679) to which he appended an essay entitled *The Grounds of Criticism in Tragedy*. Rapin and Rymer are still in the forefront of his critical thinking and his summary of the main heads in *The Poetics* would have been acceptable in any seventeenth-century salon or *ruelle*. The main departure from Aristotle is as usual the emphasis on instructing delightfully through the purgation of the passions by example:[10]

Rapin, a judicious critic, has observed from Aristotle, that pride and want of commiseration are the most predominant vices in mankind; therefore, to cure us of these two, the inventors of Tragedy have chosen to work upon two other passions, which are fear and pity. We are wrought to fear by their setting before

[10] Dryden, *Dramatic Essays*.

our eyes some terrible example of misfortune, which happened to persons of the highest quality; for such an action demonstrates to us that no condition is privileged from the turns of fortune; this must of necessity cause terror in us, and consequently abate our pride. But when we see that the most virtuous, as well as the greatest, are not exempt from such misfortunes, that consideration moves pity in us, and insensibly works us to be helpful to, and tender over, the distressed; which is the noblest and most god-like of moral virtues.   (pp. 131–2)

Dryden is at his most conservative in this essay. Having started by asking the question how far his age ought to imitate Shakespeare and Fletcher in their plots, he concludes that they are to be followed only in the excellencies which they have copied from 'those who invented and brought to perfection Dramatic Poetry'. In considering manners, the poet must first follow the advice of Le Bossu and be clear about his moral intention; he must then illustrate manners through the actions of characters who play their parts with Horatian decorum. The hero must have more of virtue in him than of vice and 'it is on this one character that pity and terror must be principally if not wholly, founded'. For character drawing, no one is better than Shakespeare, except Jonson. To illustrate Shakespeare's skill in characterisation, he chooses not a human being but the fictional monster Caliban, begotten by an incubus on a witch and showing just those qualities we would expect from such a generation. A quotation from Longinus encourages him to remind the reader of what he had clearly stated in the *Defence*, that fancy must be tempered by judgment and so the passions must be kept in control. Corneille's warning against the inappropriate expression of 'sententiae' is repeated ('No man is at leisure to make sentences and similes when his soul is in agony') and the point amusingly illustrated by a self-deprecating example from his own *The Indian Emperor.* The essay ends with what might be taken as Dryden's last word on the rules, at the very name of which some men are shocked 'as if they were a kind of magisterial prescription upon poets'. Leaning again on Rapin, he concludes: 'they are founded upon good sense, and sound reason, rather than on authority'.

These three essays, *An Essay of Dramatic Poesy, A Defence of An Essay* and *Grounds of Criticism* summarise Dryden's position as a drama critic and would seem on even the most liberal reading to place him in the seventeenth-century neo-classical tradition. And then there was the long tussle with Shakespeare. Dryden never seemed fully to apprehend that Sophocles and Shakespeare were writing different kinds of plays though he realised they were both great dramatists, nor does he seem to have been aware how very different in kind were his own adaptations of the works of both writers. In the *Preface to 'An Evening's Love'* (1671) Shakespeare is accused of 'superfluity and waste of wit'. In the *Defence of the Epilogue to the Second Part of 'The Conquest of Granada'* (1672) Shakespeare and his contemporaries are the victims of that kind of false historicism, fashionable in Dryden's day, which supported a theory of linguistic progress whereby 'an improvement of our Wit, Language and Conversation' could be taken as self-evident. Shakespeare and Fletcher were therefore guilty of solecisms in speech and notorious flaws in sense. 'But the times were ignorant in which they lived.' *Pericles,* all the histories, *The Winter's Tale, Love's Labour's Lost* and *Measure for Measure* suffered from lameness of plot. Shakespeare's audience was 'content with acorns before they knew the use of bread'. On the matter of wit, that stylistic touchstone of the period, Shakespeare 'writes in many places below the dullest writer of ours, or any precedent age'. 'Let us therefore admire the beauties and heights of Shakespeare, without following after him into a carelessness, and, as I may call it, a lethargy of thought for whole scenes together.' In spite of all this, says Dryden, he would not assume to himself the title of better poet.

Four years later, in the *Prologue to 'Aurung-Zebe'* he places Shakespeare even more positively on the heights of Parnassus:

But spite of all his pride, a secret shame
Invades his breast at *Shakespear's* sacred name:
Aw'd when he hears his Godlike *Romans* rage,
He, in a just despair, would quit the Stage
And to an Age less polish'd, more unskill'd,
Does, with disdain the foremost Honours yield.   (ll. 13–18)

The lines are followed by the comment that while he will not strive with the 'greater dead', he is not prepared to match his verse with the living:

Let him retire, betwixt two Ages cast,
The first of this, and hindmost of the last.   (ll. 21–2)

There is a truth in this for Dryden felt himself to be writing between two ages, on a literary watershed. In the context of the Battle of the Books he is far from being the clearly identifiable Modern that so many critics, including W. P. Ker, would have him.

Dryden's inability – and that of his age – to come to terms with the real nature of Shakespearian tragedy is revealed in the *Preface to 'All For Love'* as are, in the play itself, his own special strengths and weaknesses. Voicing the critical views of Le Bossu, he reckons that the fascination of the story of Antony and Cleopatra lies in 'the excellency of the moral'. In brief, this is an exemplary tale of misfortune consequent upon allowing love to come in the way of political business. Better if the

111

two had never met. 'Our passions are, or ought to be, within our power.' He congratulates himself on the formal structure of the play and requests his reader to admire the handling of the Octavia–Cleopatra confrontation. It is clear that he considers the strength of this scene to lie in what nowadays we would call its psychological realism:[11]

I judged it both natural and probable that Octavia, proud of her new-gained conquest, would search out Cleopatra to triumph over her: and that Cleopatra, thus attacked, was not of a spirit to shun the encounter: and 'tis not unlikely that two exasperated rivals should use such satire as I have put into their mouths; for, after all, though the one were a Roman, and the other a queen, they were both women.   (p. 119)

A close imitation of the responses of real people in a like situation is here his quarry. In the same vein, but tinged with that particular form of irony amounting to an intellectual sneer which he used when addressing audiences, he points out in the *Prologue* to the play that:

His Heroe, whom you Wits his Bully call,
Bates of his mettle; and scarce rants at all:
He's somewhat lewd, but a well-meaning mind;
Weeps much; fights little; but is won'drous kind.   (ll. 10–13)

The vainglorious ranting hero of earlier Restoration heroic tragedy, with his ancestry vaguely in the Tamburlaine stud book, is being replaced by a character more recognisable as an ordinary weak mortal, and the model for this kind of naturalism is to be found, he says in his closing paragraph to the *Preface*, in Shakespeare, by imitating whom he has excelled himself throughout the play. Shakespeare, as he says in the later *Grounds of Criticism in Tragedy* 'had an universal mind, which comprehended all characters and passions'.

[11] Dryden, *Dramatic Essays.*

112

And yet, this devotion to the vivid and realistic presentation of the passions was never for Dryden the ultimate aim of the highest poetry. When he came to write his *Dedication of the Aeneis* (1697) he virtually abjured tragedy in favour of the epic. The opening sentence summarises his considered opinion: 'A Heroic Poem, truly such, is undoubtedly the greatest work which the soul of man is capable to perform'. While tragedy is a miniature of human life, 'an epic poem is the draught at length'. The dwarf heroes of the theatre cannot vie with the great epic figures 'since the style of the heroic is, and ought to be, more lofty than that of the drama'. With that rapid and precise response which he had all his life to the shifting currents of contemporary opinion, Dryden senses how the theatre is moving towards naturalism and although he followed the trend in his treatment of the Antony theme, now, on reflection, he is withdrawing his support from the new theatre. By reducing Antony's status to that of a blind impassioned lover, he had followed the fashion and at the same time produced a hero who, if not a dwarf, was certainly smaller than his prototype. Dryden's poetic insight led him to a recognition of the imaginative freedom which the epic gave, or seemed to give, to the projection of grandiose superhuman beings who satisfied his conception of the ideal. The stage was harnessed to the probable and the probable in the creatural terms demanded by representation through human actors led to naturalism. In these closing years of his life, Dryden was witnessing an attack on the theatre, led by Jeremy Collier in his *A Short View of the Immorality and Prophaneness of the English Stage* which in a roundabout way encouraged the move towards naturalism since it implied that if the theatre were to have a continuing existence, it must become a centre of instruction in the current social mores rather than continue to bring in a selective soothing report about life based on the concept of 'poetical justice'.

The phrase 'poetical justice' was invented, it would seem, by Thomas Rymer (1641–1713) who began his literary career when a law student by publishing, in 1668, an anthology of the works of Cicero in English. He caught the interest of the Town with a translation of Rapin's *Reflections* in 1674, the preface to which gives an early example of his ferocious analytical method decorated by a snarling raillery, and at the same time states in clear measured terms what he considers poetry should be about. Aristotle argued inductively, establishing principles out of the practice of poets, but reasons, apart from Aristotle, are as clear as any demonstration in mathematics. Probability is the primary element in poetry for without probability, poetry has no life, is inoperant. The argument is continued in *Tragedies of the Last Age* (1678) but here he is less favourably disposed towards the English dramatists, who, if they had been wise, should have built on the model of Sophocles or Euripides. He is going to concern himself chiefly with the fable or plot which as has been said is the soul of tragedy. Common sense will lead to a proper judgment of the plot and common sense is merely the application of Reason, no matter what some people may say about poetry being the child of Fancy:[12]

Say others, *Poetry* and *Reason*, how come these to be Cater-cousins? Poetry is the *Child* of *Fancy* and is never to be school'd and disciplin'd by *Reason*; Poetry, say they, is *blind* inspiration, is pure *enthusiasm*, is *rapture* and *rage* all over.

But *Fancy*, I think, in Poetry, is like *Faith* in Religion: it makes far discoveries, and soars above reason, but never clashes or

---

[12] Quotations from Spingarn, *Critical Essays*, vol. ii. The use of italics follows the original. One assumes Rymer wrote as if he heard himself pleading at the Bar.

runs against it. *Fancy* leaps and frisks, and away she's gone, whilst *reason* rattles the chains and follows after. *Reason* must consent and ratify what-ever by *fancy* is attempted in its absence, or else 'tis all *null* and void in law. However, in the contrivance and *oeconomy* of a play *reason* is always principally to be consulted. Those who object against reason are the *Fanaticks* in Poetry, and are never to be sav'd by their good works. (p. 185)

Some things in the fictional world of drama are, according to Rymer, reasonable, others are not. The action must be probable and this kind of probability postulates a certain limited area within which the characters of drama can function if they are to retain the credibility of reasonable people. So we learn that kings should not be an accessory to a crime; poetry will not permit an affront where there can be no reparation; tragedy cannot represent a woman without modesty; in poetry no woman is to kill a man nor is a servant to kill the master. 'Poetical decency will not suffer death to be dealt to each other by such persons whom the Laws of Duel allow not to enter the lists together.' In this highly artificial world – where Chapelain would have felt quite at home – all behaviour should illustrate that special type of justice known as poetical justice:[13]

And besides the *purging* of the *passions*, something must stick by observing that constant order, that harmony and beauty of Providence, that necessary relation and chain, whereby the causes and the effects, the vertues and rewards, the vices and their punishments, are proportion'd and link'd together, how deep and dark soever are laid the Springs and however intricate and involv'd are their operations. (pp. 206–7)

*A Short View of Tragedy* (1693) adds little novelty to Rymer's general approach. He is pleased that Racine has revived the chorus though his arguments in favour are

[13] Spingarn, *Critical Essays.*

unexpected, for he maintains that the chorus benefits the spectators in so far as it helps to establish a just and reasonable basis for the time and place of the representation and it benefits the poet because it provides a goodly show, so he will not require to rack his wits for 'some foreign Toy or Hobby-horse to humour the Multitude'. He agrees that a play should satisfy the eyes and ears of the audience but too often audiences ask for nothing more, to the detriment of plot, character, any sense or any wise word. On the other hand, some poets, such as Shakespeare and Ben Jonson, use too many words. 'In a play one should speak like a man of business.' The notorious reading, or misreading, of *Othello* included in this essay is a masterpiece of unconstructive critical butchery, but given Rymer's initial postulates regarding the nature of tragedy, his conclusions are logical enough. If one looks for a tight structure innocent of any improbabilities, a clearly defined time-scale within the twenty-four hour bracket, and a moral demonstrating that the wicked are punished and the good rewarded, one will seek in vain for these qualities in *Othello*. Rymer saw this and said so. From one point of view he might be praised for his critical awareness in appreciating what Dryden never fully apprehended, that the neo-classical prescript could not be adapted to suit Elizabethan or Jacobean tragedy. The conduct of the plot in *Othello* is, in neo-classical terms, neither probable, natural nor reasonable. In this play there can be no 'instruction' for the audience, either in Shakespeare's time, in Rymer's, or in ours. Iago is certainly a monster and the implied negative in answer to the question: 'If this be our end, what boots it to be Vertuous?' is a correct assessment of the audience's response to the play. Dryden's statement that 'I reverence Mr Rymer's learning' and Pope's judgment on him as 'on the whole one of the best critics we have ever had' indicate how suitably, and ably, he expressed the accepted critical commonplaces of his day. He aligns himself with the ancients, unperturbed by the cry for 'progress' which was spreading from the scientific to the literary world.

An immediate commentary on *A Short View of Tragedy* came from John Dennis (1657–1734) in the form of a series of dialogues entitled *The Impartial Critic* (1693). Using material closely derived from Dacier, whom he holds to be 'the best commentator on Aristotle', Dennis considers the case for and against the use of the chorus and concludes with a total rejection of Rymer's views on this topic. In his introductory *Letter* he accuses Rymer of endeavouring to force the Grecian method on English drama in defiance of the difference in religion, polity and climate. In whatever spirit the Greeks accepted the chorus, today in England it is neither probable nor natural. Nor is the Greek attitude to sex and to love tolerable in this age and country.

In the *Second Dialogue*, Dennis compares Dryden's presentation of the character of Oedipus with that of Sophocles, to the detriment of the former. He approves Dacier's straightforward moralistic interpretation of catharsis. Sophocles' *Oedipus Rex* is about a man who failed to look to his weaknesses, just as the audience neglect their own passions and frailties, so let them take heed:[14]

Beaumont: Why, will you perswade me that because an Audience finds in itself the same vain Curiosity and the same ungovern'd Passions that drew *Oedipus* to murder and incest, that therefore each Spectator should be afraid of killing his Father and committing Incest with his Mother?

Freeman: No, you cannot mistake me so far; but they may very well be afraid of being drawn in by the like neglected

[14] Spingarn, *Critical Essays*, vol. III.

Passions to deplorable Crimes and horrid Mischiefs which they never design'd.   (p. 164)

Dryden erred in describing an Oedipus who was 'Soveraignly Vertuous, and guilty of Parricide only by a fatal invincible Ignorance'. This can raise neither terror nor pity but only horror. Once again, one notices how the early moralistic reading of Aristotle gains a new lease of life by mutation into the doctrine of poetical justice, implying the confirmation of a moral universe. Dryden's version of the king's story, in Dennis's view, is altered for the worse because Oedipus shows frailties rather than faults and so is unjustly punished, but even Aristotle would admit that Dryden had written a 'beautiful' play.

The fourth and fifth dialogues return again to the theme of the chorus. Once the discussion moves beyond the appeal of authority – Dacier on the one hand, Rymer on the other – it develops into a confrontation between the demands of verisimilitude and the advantages of a unified structure which will make the play into a satis-factory whole, one and entire. First, the 'absurdity' of the chorus:[15]

But suppose we had Charity to grant that it is impossible for a grave and important Action to be acted in publick by great Men, but others must intermeddle in it: Can *Dacier* infer from hence that these people thus concerned ought to sing and dance at their Princes Sufferings? I will grant it probable that at the suffering of Kings several should be concern'd; at the same time you must grant it absurd that they should sing and dance at their Sufferings. Now, would you have a Poet shew a thing that's absurd to shew something else that is probable, when the probability may be suppos'd as well as shewn, or shewn without an absurdity?   (p. 190)

As a specific example of absurdity in a Greek play, he refers to Sophocles' *Electra*:

[15] Spingarn, vol. III.

The absurdity which I speak of is the discovery that *Orestes* makes of himself and his design to *Electra* in the Fourth Act of that Tragedy, which he does in the presence of the Chorus; so that he entrusts a Secret, upon which his Empire and Life depends, in the hands of Sixteen Women. For *Orestes* had no Friends on whose assistance he might rely, unless it were his Friend and his Governour, and consequently he had nothing to depend upon but Secresie and Surprize and a swift Execution. (p. 192)

On the contrary side, his interlocutor reminds him:

*Beaumont:* A Tragedy, said he, is the imitation of an Action, which must be one and entire; and therefore there must be a Chorus: For without it the Acts can never be joyn'd, there will be a solution of continuity, and Tragedy can never be one entire Body. When the stage is left empty upon the end of the First Act, what grounds has a company to believe the actors will return? (pp. 193–4)

To this the answer is:

*Freeman:* The Rules of *Aristotle* are nothing but Nature and Good Sence reduc'd to a Method. I may very well suppose that every one Who goes to see a Tragedy acted goes with a hope that he shall not see something absurd, and that he has common Sence to know that a Tragedy would be very absurd which should conclude abruptly before the just end of the Action; that is to say, before that part of it which necessarily supposes nothing to follow it. (pp. 194–5)

This appeal to good sense rouses Beaumont to question the use of fiddlers between the acts. Are they not even more absurd and unnatural? They may be, agrees Freeman, but then they are not an essential part of the tragedy. They do not interfere with its unity because they are not part of its structure and nothing can be more structurally divisive than an absurd chorus. 'For Poetry, being an imitation of Nature, anything which is un-

119

natural strikes at the very Root and Being of it, and ought to be avoided like Ruine.' The argument is by now a familiar one. How close must the imitation be to 'nature' in order that the reason of the audience will be encouraged to accept the events on the stage as if they were really happening?

Those historians of English literature who would interpret the eighteenth century as a period of gradual disengagement from the domination of the neo-classical rules leading to the blessed relaxes and creative freedom of the 'Romantic Revival' seize on *A Discourse Upon Comedy* (1702) by George Farquhar (1678–1707) as an early manifesto announcing the new dawn. Close examination of the text however reveals that it could hardly be interpreted as a revolutionary document. By the time he wrote his *Discourse* Farquhar was twenty-four and had written four comparatively successful plays, although his two best, *The Recruiting Officer* and *The Beaux' Stratagem* were still to come. He begins his essay by mocking the rule-bound dramatist in a kind of parody of Rymer's style though Rymer would hardly accept the implications:[16]

So to work he goes; old Aristotle, Scaliger, with their commentators, are lugged down from the high shelf, and the moths are dislodged from their tenement of years; Horace, Vossius, Heinsius, Hedelin, Rapin, with some half a dozen more, are thumbed and tossed about to teach the gentleman, forsooth, to write a comedy; and here is he furnished with Unity of Action, Continuity of Action, Extent of Time, Preparation of Incidents, Episodes, Narrations, Deliberations, Didactics, Pathetics, Monologues, Figures, Intervals, Castastrophes, Choruses, Scenes, Machines, Decorations, &c. – a stock sufficient to set up any mountebank in Christendom. And if our new author would take an opportunity of reading a lecture upon his play in these terms, by the help of a zany and a joint-stool, his scenes might

[16] Quotations from *Eighteenth Century Critical Essays*, ed. Scott Elledge.

go off as well as the doctors' packets; but the misfortune of it is, he scorns all application to the vulgar, and will please the better sort, as he calls his own sort. Pursuant, therefore, to his philosophical dictates, he first chooses a single plot, because most agreeable to the regularity of criticism, no matter whether it affords business enough for diversion or surprise. He would not for the world introduce a song or dance, because his play must be one entire action. We must expect no variety of incidents, because the exactness of his three hours won't give him time for their preparation. The Unity of Place admits no variety of painting and prospect, by which mischance, perhaps, we shall lose the only good scenes in the play. But no matter for that; this play is a regular play; this play has been examined and approved by such and such gentlemen, who are stanch critics, and masters of art; and this play I will have acted. Lookee, Mr Rich, you may venture to lay out a hundred and fifty pound for dressing this play, for it was written by a great scholar, and fellow of a college.

Then a grave dogmatical prologue is spoken to instruct the audience what should please them; that this play has a new and different cut from the farce they see every day; that this author writes after the manner of the Ancients, and here is a piece according to the model of the Athenian drama. Very well! This goes off, Hum drum, so-so. Then the players go to work on a piece of hard, knotty stuff, where they can no more show their art, than a carpenter can upon a piece of steel. Here is the lamp and the scholar in every line, but not a syllable of the poet. Here is elaborate language, sounding epithets, flights of words that strike the clouds, whilst the poor sense lags after, like the lanthorn in the tail of the kite, which appears only like a star while the breath of the players' lungs has strength enough to bear it up in the air.   (pp. 82–3)

Having enjoyed his critical 'horseplay, Farquhar continues in a more muted, even traditional, tone with a definition of comedy as 'a well-framed tale handsomely told as an agreeable vehicle for counsel or reproof' and 'an art of schooling mankind into better manners'. He repeats the view expressed by Dryden and Dennis that 'an English play is intended for the use and instruction of an English audience' therefore 'the rules of an English comedy do not lie in the compass of Aristotle or his followers but in the pit, box and galleries'. The unities of time and place are likely targets for censure even although the young critic admits to working fairly closely within them in his own plays. His argument follows the lines of Howard's extreme statement in the *Lerma Preface*, his words even echoing those of Howard's: 'For that a thousand years should come within the compass of three hours is no more an impossibility than that two minutes should be contained in one'. On place he makes a similar and by no means novel comment and concludes this essay disarmingly by saying he is 'as little a friend to those rambling plays as anybody'. On the other hand he finds it necessary to say something 'in vindication of the great Shakespeare' who, being a poet, which Aristotle was not, was therefore the greater critic.

Farquhar plants his essay firmly on neo-classical terrain by concluding that our English authors are guilty of faults only 'if they have left vice unpunished, virtue unrewarded, folly unexposed, or prudence unsuccessful, the contrary of which is the *Utile* of comedy' or 'if any part of their plots have been independent of the rest, or any of their characters forced or unnatural, which destroys the *Dulce* of plays'. He continues:[17]

But if by a true decorum in these material points, they have writ successfully and answered the end of dramatic poetry in every respect, let them rest in peace, and their memories enjoy the encomium due to their merit.   (p. 86)

Such Horatian insistence on the *Utile* and the *Dulce* would suggest that the neo-classical doctrine was every bit

[17] Elledge, *Critical Essays*.

as firmly entrenched at the beginning of the new century
as it had been in the days of the early Dryden. The central
belief of seventeenth-century dramatic theory remains
unchallenged, that the play is an idealised reflection of
human life calculated to move an audience into a state of
self-awareness leading to self-examination and moral
improvement, this last only being possible if the degree of
idealisation does not overstep the bonds of credibility
while, at the same time, and in order that the moral lesson
may be inculcated, interest must be maintained in
tragedy by an infusion of the marvellous, and in comedy
by the fascination of a complicated intrigue. The
dilemma of endeavouring to provide an exemplary
pattern of behaviour while at the same time truly
representing nature as evinced in the actions of men
remains unresolved, unless one takes refuge in that
kind of circular argument which holds that probability
('vraisemblance') is a general interpretation of nature
which is acceptable to reason and reason is that faculty in
man which recognises the inherent applicability of the
probable in a given situation. The problem peculiar to
English criticism, which Farquhar appreciated up to a
point when he juxtaposed the two names, was the
reconciliation of Aristotle with Shakespeare. The growth
of the historical method revealed possibilities but eventually became too simple a solution when everything in
Shakespeare which did not seem to comply with the rules
was attributed to the barbarity of his age. Eighteenth-
century English critics were in no doubt that he was
the great master of portraying passion and delineating
human characters in all their 'natural' variety. Subsequent criticism will tend to base a theory on the preponderance of character over action so that the work of
Shakespeare, and, by extension, all drama will be valued
for its power to reveal the mysteries of the human soul.

# 5

# Rowe, Pope and Johnson on Shakespeare

Restoration playwrights, critics and audiences encouraged a climate of opinion which ensured the acceptance of Shakespeare as the central figure in the English literary tradition, and his placing was confirmed by the rise of the Shakespeare editing industry. It was assumed, correctly, that the available texts were corrupt, carelessly prepared for the press and printed in a state of disarray. The least homage that could be offered to the native poet was therefore to treat him as a modern classic and bring his works in front of the public in new and corrected versions. The prefaces attached to these many editions are a guide to the critical attitudes adopted towards Shakespeare throughout the century, attitudes and responses based on a set of assumptions which in their turn derived from what might be called the anglicisation of the neo-classical rules.

The first criterion to which Shakespeare measured up admirably was the degree of verisimilitude in the plays. The poet reflected nature so that all men might say they here beheld themselves – or some abstraction which they could liken to themselves – in action. The eighteenth century was an age concerned to make and hear statements about the condition, the potential and the complexity of the human species and these were questions which had exercised the attention of Shakespeare to the point where it could be demonstrated, in the words of Maurice Morgann, that his characters were 'rather historic than dramatic beings'. Such an opinion would have evoked from Castelvetro a sagacious nod of approval.

The second principle in neo-classical doctrine which appealed to the eighteenth century was the need for form, for decorum, for an approved procedure, efficient, reasonable and permanent, equally applicable to the conduct of literature and the conduct of society. In literature, tradition encouraged a reliance on the creed of Aristotle and Horace, as later interpreted. The formula, on the face of it, seemed reliable, well-tried and based on common sense. But here came the rub – Shakespeare either knew nothing of it, or if he did, he spurned it, for he mixed comedy with tragedy and beggars with aristocrats; of the unities, except in *The Tempest*, and one or two other less popular plays, he seemed hardly to have heard and even his language frequently lacked that elevation of style, that vibrant splendour which alone should be deemed a suitable vehicle for the tragic experience. So we find that much of the dialogue between Shakespeare and his critics consists of their excusing his 'faults' by the application of a false historicism: he lived in barbarous times, spoke a less refined vernacular, shared the company of coarse players, and so on. The approach is once again a repetition and reinforcement of arguments first proposed by Dryden, whose appetite for 'refinement' found little sustenance in Shakespeare.

The third bastion of neo-classical criticism, rejuvenated by the invention of the phrase 'poetical justice', supported the 'art and morality' argument that the poet, along with the priest and the philosopher is given the task of indicating the way to the good life. In so far as Shakespeare shows a concern for particular lives and unique people struggling in a complex of external obligations, he satisfies the moral demands made of him

5-2

as a poet, but his judgments are often misguided, for, in Johnson's phrasing: 'he makes no just distribution of good and evil, nor is always careful to show in the virtuous a disapprobation of the wicked'. Addison is almost alone in going against the general trend when, in Spectator no. 40 (Monday, 16 April 1711) he writes:[1]

The English writers of tragedy are possessed with a notion, that when they represent a virtuous or innocent person in distress, they ought not to leave him till they have delivered him out of his troubles, or made him triumph over his enemies. This error they have been led into by a ridiculous doctrine in modern criticism, that they are obliged to an equal distribution of rewards and punishments, and an impartial execution of poetical justice. Who were the first that established this rule I know not; but I am sure it has no foundation in nature, in reason, or in the practice of the ancients. We find that good and evil happen alike to all men on this side the grave; and as the principal design of tragedy is to raise commiseration and terror in the minds of the audience, we shall defeat this great end, if we always make virtue and innocence happy and successful. (p. 146)

One of the earliest eighteenth-century editors was Nicholas Rowe who brought out an edition of *The Works* in 1709 prefaced by *Some Account of the Life etc. of Mr. William Shakespear*. Rowe agrees with Addison in condemning tragi-comedy reluctantly conceding that it would seem to be a form agreeable to the English taste and one to which Shakespeare was addicted. He then goes on to set the critical style for the century by extrapolating from the plays those characters with whom he finds himself most in sympathy – Falstaff, Malvolio, Shylock, among others – and providing brief appreciations. *The Tempest* is particularly praised for its adherence to the unities and for the inclusion of the grotesque

[1] Addison, *The Spectator with Sketches of the Lives of the Authors.*

126

Caliban, a figure whom no eighteenth-century critic encountered without admiration. There follows what is to become another commonplace of Augustan and later criticism, the confrontation of Aristotle and Shakespeare, wherein the latter is excused liability for ignoring the precepts of the former, because he knew no better:[2]

If one undertook to examine the greatest part of these by those Rules which are establish'd by *Aristotle*, and taken from the model of the *Grecian* stage, it would be no very hard Task to find a great many Faults: But as *Shakespear* liv'd under a kind of mere Light of Nature, and had never been made acquainted with the Regularity of those written Precepts, so it would be hard to judge him by a Law he knew nothing of. We are to consider him as a Man that liv'd in a State of almost universal Licence and Ignorance: There was no establish'd Judge, but everyone took the liberty to Write according to the Dictates of his own Fancy. When one considers, that there is not one play before him of a Reputation good enough to entitle it to an Appearance on the present Stage, it cannot but be a Matter of great Wonder that he should advance Dramatick Poetry so far as he did.   (p. 15)

Shakespeare, he continues, was not very strong on plot and structure (the unities again) but made 'recompense for his carelessness in this point' in the excellence of his character drawing. Henry VI, Henry VIII, Queen Katherine, Coriolanus, Brutus and Marc Antony are paraded as examples, the last two, as he says, very close to their originals in Plutarch, from whom Shakespeare has taken more incident than he need have done, for 'his Design seems most commonly rather to describe those great Men in the several Fortunes and Accidents of their Lives, than to take any single great Action, and form his Work simply upon that'. However, some of the plays are founded on one action only and among these is *Hamlet*.

[2] All quotations in this chapter are from *Eighteenth Century Essays on Shakespeare*, ed. D. Nichol Smith.

Here follows an ingenious comparison between *Hamlet* and Sophocles' *Electra* to the detriment of the latter:[3]

*Orestes* embrues his Hands in the blood of his own Mother... While *Electra*, her Daughter, and a Princess, both of them Characters that ought to have appear'd with more Decency, stands upon the Stage and encourages her Brother in the Parricide. What Horror does this not raise!... to represent an Action of this Kind on the Stage, is certainly an Offence against those Rules of Manners proper to the Persons that ought to be observ'd there. On the contrary, let us only look a little on the Conduct of *Shakespeare*. *Hamlet* is represented with the same Piety towards his Father, and Resolution to Revenge his Death, as *Orestes*; he has the same Abhorrence for his Mother's Guilt, which, to provoke him the more, is heighten'd by Incest: But 'tis with wonderful Art and Justness of Judgment that the Poet restrains him from doing Violence to his Mother. To prevent anything of that Kind, he makes his Father's Ghost forbid that part of his Vengeance. This is to distinguish rightly between *Horror* and *Terror*. The latter is a proper Passion of Tragedy, but the former ought always to be carefully avoided. (p. 18)

Rowe's essay is a sensitive discussion of some of the durable qualities in Shakespeare, expressed in the manner and style of Dryden and continuing the earlier critic's method of using the old prescriptive doctrine as a norm, but excusing the poet when he departs from it on the grounds that he cannot be held responsible for failing to conform to 'a Law he knew nothing of'. The 'written Precepts' as Rowe calls them continue to be the touchstone by which drama will be tested and in fairness to the authors of these precepts, one might ask whether their 'rules' did not in fact form a valuable basis for a reasoned consideration of the meaning, methods and aims of comedy and tragedy as literary genres, even although

[3] Nichol Smith, *Eighteenth Century Essays.*

their relevance to the work of the one outstanding master of the English theatre could be validated only after considerable qualifications. The question arises whether a partially appropriate critical system is better than no system at all (assuming that criticism is accepted on any terms as a profitable exercise) or, in historical terms, whether nineteenth-century criticism of Shakespeare made any great advance on that of the previous century. The virtue of the best eighteenth-century critics resides in their ability to use a procedure without being dominated by it, nor are they or the procedure to be condemned on account of the footling noises made by the Dick Minims of the age.

Pope's *Preface* (1725) to his text of Shakespeare disclaims any concern for offering a critique, and merely provides a few desultory comments on the 'principal and characteristic Excellencies' which are subsumed under the two well-established headings of Characterisation and Power over the Passions. Originality is also granted to Shakespeare in the frequently quoted passage: 'The Poetry of Shakespeare was Inspiration indeed: he is not so much an Imitator as an Instrument of Nature; and 't is not so just to say that he speaks from her, as that she speaks thro' him.'[4] This could be read to mean that Shakespeare has transcended mere imitation, that he has gone beyond an interpretation of the common field of human experience which the eighteenth century called nature, and has, after the manner of Sidney's metaphor, conjured up a golden world, a world that in experiential terms neither is nor is not ('The symbol neither is nor is not the reality which it manifests.')[5] But his subsequent remarks imply that he is merely repeating in emphatic terms the established view that Shakespeare's character-

---

[4] Nichol Smith, *Eighteenth Century Essays*, p. 44.
[5] Northrop Frye, *Anatomy of Criticism*, p. 351.

isation is good because it is lifelike; it is individualised and it is consistent, drawn from the life and not from other writers.

The influence of the now fashionable Longinian trend of thought is obvious in Pope's remarks on Shakespeare's 'Power over our Passions'. 'But the heart swells, and the tears burst out, just at the proper places.'[6] What the proper places are we are not told but we seem to be moving away from structural analysis, centred for instance on a consideration of the placing and use of the cathartic device or the significance of tension and conflict. It is enough that the dramatist should move us to tears whenever he so intends regardless of the total plan or purpose. We are not so far away from that lachrymose stage in critical evaluation when tears become in themselves a good thing.

Following accepted practice, Pope now turns to a consideration of the poet's faults. Most of these are due to the Elizabethan audience, mean people enjoying comedies involving tradesmen and mechanics and full of buffoonery, ribaldry and unmannerly jests. The plots of the history plays follow vulgar traditions and even tragedy is vitiated by strange, unexpected, unnatural events and incidents, exaggerated thoughts, verbose and bombastic expression, pompous rhymes and thundering versification. However, our dramatist negotiates these low parts 'like some Prince of Romance in the disguise of a Shepherd or Peasant'.[7]

To judge therefore of *Shakespear* by *Aristotle's* rules, is like trying a man by the Laws of one Country, who acted under those of another. He writ to the *People*; and writ at first without patronage from the better sort, and therefore without aims of pleasing them: without assistance or advice from the Learned,

[6] Nichol Smith, *Eighteenth Century Essays*, p. 45.
[7] Nichol Smith, *Eighteenth Century Essays*, p. 47.

as without the advantage of education or acquaintance among them: without that knowledge of the best models, the Ancients, to inspire him with an emulation of them; in a word, without any views of Reputation, and of what Poets are pleas'd to call Immortality: Some or all of which have encourag'd the vanity, or animated the ambition, of other writers.   (p. 47)

Shakespeare would have avoided the worst of his faults if he had not been obliged to pander to an ignorant audience or keep company with coarse actors. Contrary to some views, he was not devoid of learning. 'Nothing is more evident than that he had a taste of natural Philosophy, Mechanics, ancient and modern History, Poetical learning and Mythology' (p. 49). With some shrewdness, Pope decides that the myth of Shakespeare's unlettered condition stemmed from those partisans who would elevate him above Ben Jonson and who therefore maintained that because Shakespeare had the more wit and fancy, he needed not the learning of Jonson – the primitive versus the sophisticate.

Neither Pope's critical techniques as applied to Shakespeare nor his conclusions have moved beyond those of Dryden. There is the same urge to apply the neo- classical doctrine in its entirety coupled with a clear apprehension that this procedure results in value judgments which are at odds with the felt response to the poetry. So the procedure is modified to include explanations which provoke further artificial and peripheral problems, such as those associated with his audience, his sources or his personal social milieu. If the traditional criticism were to be used on Shakespeare – and no one seemed as yet able or ready to invent a better – it would have to be used by a critic who would appreciate that a literal application of the doctrine, no matter how sanctified, led to serious blockages and must in some manner be circumvented, for it was clear that Shakespeare and undiluted neo-classicism could not cohabit. So far, the most that critics could say was that Shakespeare did not share the same frame of reference as the sixteenth-century scholars who laid the foundations for the rules, but nonetheless he wrote not badly, despite his ignorance of the tradition. In mid-eighteenth century, Samuel Johnson (1709–1784) turned his energetic mind to the problem.

Criticism, says Johnson in *Rambler* no. 3 dated Tuesday, 27 March 1750, was the daughter of Labour and Truth, adopted by Justice and brought up in the palace of Wisdom. Weary of attending on the doubtful claims of mortals, she eventually handed the task of judging to Time under whose slow proceedings many claimants to fame have been forgotten. So Criticism handed over to Time and left Prejudice and False Taste to ravage at large as the associates of Fraud and Mischief. In the long run, the final true judgment still rests with Time. Four days later, on Saturday March 31st (*Rambler* no. 4) he told his readers that:

the works of fiction with which the present generation seems more particularly delighted, are such as exhibit life in its true state, diversified only by accidents that daily happen in the world, and influenced by passions and qualities which are really to be found in conversing with mankind. This kind of writing may be termed not improperly the comedy of romance, and is to be conducted nearly by the rules of comic poetry.

In so far as these writers have to engage in general converse and accurate observation of the living world, being just copiers of human manners, they are to be commended far above the writers of the old 'heroic romance' who surrounded themselves with giants, knights, deserts, castles, hermits, woods, battles and shipwrecks. But, and this minatory 'but' although he does not tell us so is a consequence of his recent perusal of

*Roderick Random* and *Tom Jones*, 'these books are written chiefly to the young, the ignorant and the idle to whom they serve as lectures of conduct and introductions into life'. Shades of Castelvetro and J. C. Scaliger! 'Such novels,' he continues, 'may convey the knowledge of vice and virtue with more efficacy than axioms or definitions'. Their authors, while imitating nature, must select from nature those individuals upon which the attention ought most to be employed. Real life is often discoloured by passion or deformed by wickedness and so a promiscuous description of the real world is no part of the writer's contractual obligation. Many characters ought never to be drawn. Some are drawn with a mingling of good and bad qualities (alas, poor Tom Jones!) so that 'we lose the abhorrence of their faults'. So it is the primacy of fiction as against history that fiction can and should exhibit the most perfect idea of virtue – a sentiment at which neither Robertello nor Minturno would have been able to cavil.

A year later, on 28 May 1751 (*Rambler* no. 125) his readers were warned that definitions are hazardous, are not the province of man, are a defiance of that relativity at the heart of nature and the arts. Comedy for instance, how can it be defined? 'Such a dramatic representation of human life, as may excite mirth.' It had been better if tragedy and comedy had been defined only by their effects upon the mind, then we should have been spared the fallacy of tragedy being identified with high life and comedy with low. This essay concludes with a tendentious analysis of part of a scene from Dryden's *Aurung-Zebe* ('in this scene every circumstance concurs to turn tragedy to farce') and the muted commendation of contemporary tragedians 'that they avoid gross faults and that if they cannot often move terror or pity, they are always careful not to provoke laughter'.

As definitions are laid waste by the relativity of life, so

laws are corrupted by error and confusion. *Rambler* no. 156 divides laws into two groups: the fundamental and indispensable dictated by reason and necessity, conforming to the order of nature and operations of the intellect; and the second group: useful, convenient or enacted by despotic antiquity or formed by accident or instituted by example. In the second group Johnson places the 'rule' that only three speaking personages appear at once upon the stage; the division into five acts; the unity of time and – the one occasion where in this group he departs from Aristotle – the rule against mixing tragedy and comedy, although even here he is by no means convinced that this is a bad rule and when broken perhaps best broken by geniuses like Shakespeare. Among the 'fixed and obligatory' rules he places unity of action and the need to have only one hero. He concludes by reminding writers that nature responding to the dictates of right reason must be distinguished from custom exemplified in 'rules which no literary dictator had authority to enact'. Johnson returns to the question of rules in *Rambler* no. 176 where they are defined as 'the instruments of mental vision, which may indeed assist our faculties when properly used, but produce confusion and obscurity by unskilful application'. The critic should be concerned about 'the justness of the design, the general spirit of the performance, the artifice of connection or the harmony of the parts':

Nothing which reason condemns can be suitable to the dignity of the human mind. To be driven by external motives from the path which our own heart approves; to give way to anything but conviction; to suffer the opinion of others to rule our choice, or overpower our resolves; is to submit tamely to the lowest and most ignominious slavery, and to resign the right of directing our own lives. (*Rambler* no. 185)

Those remarks are offered in the context of man ordering his personal affairs but they are equally applicable, in Johnson's view, to the critic ordering his judgments on literature. Johnson never questioned the validity or origin of this 'Reason' which lay behind all his moral and literary speculation; that it was for instance the product of a complex cultural heritage which included language acquisition, religious instruction, access to earlier literature and involvement in a unique society at a particular time. Enough for him that reason could be taken as a universal from which all essential principles of living could be deduced. Among those principles are a number which apply to the social activity of that class of people known as writers. Writers should (a) be concerned with the encouragement of virtue and the condemnation of vice; (b) give pleasure through a close imitation of real life to the point where every man may recognise himself (in Dacier's words: 'It is not Oedipus or Atreus or Thyestes but an ordinary man to whom one gives whatever name one likes'); (c) ensure that their inventions add up to a general view of mankind, so that when all the details of the author's biography, the expectations of his audience, the commonplaces of his age, are disposed of, there remains a residue of universal statement, or again in Dacier's words: 'a universal fable which concerns all men in general'.

Nothing that Johnson said in the *Rambler* or later in the Shakespeare *Preface* is contradicted or qualified in the two oft-quoted Dick Minim essays (*The Idler*, nos. 60 and 61). These are occasional pieces written in that tone of ironical fun over which Johnson had complete control when he was in the mood. He signals his intention in the opening sentence of no. 60: 'Criticism is a study by which men grow important and formidable at a very small expense'. We cannot but applaud the range of Dick's reading. He has Dryden, Dennis, Rymer, Farquhar, Addison and Pope – especially Pope – at his finger-tips. A cursory reading of these two essays might encourage the view that Johnson opposes all those commonplaces which he puts into Dick's mouth and which are made to look ridiculous by removal from their contexts but obviously this is not his intention. Dick's commonplaces are not necessarily bad in themselves but they are bad coming from him because he uses them as a debased false coinage, not bearing his own individual stamp. This was the kind of parrot pseudo-criticism which Johnson would not tolerate.

In the *Preface* to his edition of Shakespeare, Johnson sets out from the position he had established in *Rambler* no. 3 that 'Criticism referred the cause to be considered by Time'. 'What has been longest known has been most considered and what is most considered is best understood.' Shakespeare has begun to assume the dignity of an ancient and it is proper to enquire by what peculiarities he has kept the favour of his countrymen. In the first place, Shakespeare has given us a just representation of general nature, a mirror of manners and of life, a wide extension of design, providing practical axioms and domestic wisdom, indeed a very system of civil and economical prudence. So far, there is nothing in this with which either Horace or Scaliger would quarrel. To teach, to delight, to move, would still seem to be in the Johnsonian view the triple function of the dramatist. Nor need the affections always be concerned with love:[8]

But love is only one of many passions; and as it has no great influence upon the sum of life, it has little operation in the dramas of a poet, who caught his ideas from the living world, and exhibited only what he saw before him.   (p. 108)

[8]   Nichol Smith, *Eighteenth Century Essays.*

Surely here Johnson is applying some peculiar semantic shift to the word 'love' (e.g. a reduction to 'romantic love', 'courtly love', 'heroic love') or he is deliberately ignoring all the comedies and four out of the seven major tragedies.

Shakespeare has no heroes:

His scenes are occupied only by men, who act and speak as the reader thinks that he should himself have spoken or acted on the same occasion. Even where the agency is supernatural the dialogue is level with life. (p. 108)

He has previously said that Shakespeare's dialogue:

is pursued with so much ease and simplicity, that it seems scarcely to claim the merit of fiction, but to have been gleaned by diligent selection out of common conversation, and common occurrences. (p. 107)

This is going further than Dacier's 'we are the people he is representing'. Not only are we presented with a situation with which we may sympathise and identify, but the situation must declare itself in everyday locutions. Art is now being democratised. A courtly audience, surrounded by emblems, allegorical devices and behavioural gestures indicative of a power hierarchy naturally accepted the conventions of stage action and poetic language but now the bourgeois audience for whom Johnson is speaking asks for an imitation of life which will be as close to life itself as the linguistic and spatial demands of the stage will permit. Poetry is soon to be forbidden entry to the theatre and during this transitional period in the latter half of the eighteenth century Shakespeare is accepted on the conditions laid down by the age, conditions which arise out of the demand that all characters be psychologically integrated, complete, acceptable as 'real people'. This demand was aptly summed up by D. Nicol Smith as late as 1923 when he criticses Warton for treating Shakespeare's characters from without:[9]

> He lacks the intuitive sympathy which is the secret of later criticism. To him the play is a representation of life, not a transcript from life. The characters, who are more real to us than actual persons of history, and more intimate than many an acquaintance, appear to him to be creatures of the imagination who live in a different world from his own. Warton describes the picture: he criticizes the portraits of the characters rather than the characters themselves.

Johnson would have been in full accord with Nichol Smith, as would Pope ('His characters are so much Nature her self that it is a sort of injury to call them by so distant a name as Copies of her').

If we come to terms with Johnson's assumption concerning the need for drama to be the mirror of life, for characters to be men who 'act and speak as the reader thinks that he should himself have spoken or acted' and for dialogue to operate at the level of life, the central section of the *Preface* explains itself with little difficulty. He is answering those critics who censure Shakespeare for mixing comic and tragic scenes. Defying the traditional categories, he claims that Shakespeare's plays are neither tragedies nor comedies but 'compositions of a distinct kind', i.e. tragicomedies. Life is a mixture of good and evil, joy and sorrow, gains and losses. The ancients separated the mixture into the tragic and the comic. Shakespeare has brought them together again and in so doing has demonstrated a true dramatic kinship with nature:

> That this is a practice contrary to the rules of criticism will readily be allowed; but there is always an appeal open from

[9] Nichol Smith, *Eighteenth Century Essays*, Introduction, pp. xxxii–xxxiii.

criticism to nature. The end of writing is to instruct; the end of
poetry is to instruct by pleasing. That the mingled drama may
convey all the instruction of tragedy or comedy cannot be
denied, because it includes both in its alterations of exhibi-
tion and approaches nearer than either to the appearance of
life, by showing how great machinations and slender designs
may promote or obviate one another, and the high and the
low co-operate in the general system by unavoidable
concatenation.   (p. 110)

Tragicomedy approaches nearer to the appearance of
life; structurally it has the advantage of bringing variety
into dramatic fiction. 'Upon the whole, all pleasure
consists in variety.' And this was Shakespeare's plan, to
present 'an interchange of seriousness and merriment,
by which the mind is softened at one time and exhilarated
at another'. In his age Shakespeare met no obstacles to
the furtherance of his plan:

*Shakespeare* engaged in dramatick poetry with the world open
before him; the rules of the ancients were yet known to few; the
publick judgment was unformed; he had no example of such
fame as might force upon him imitation, nor criticks of such
authority as might restrain his extravagance: He therefore
indulged his natural disposition, and his disposition, as *Rhymer*
has remarked, led him to comedy. In tragedy he often writes
with great appearance of toil and study, what is written at last
with little felicity; but in his comick scenes, he seems to produce
without labour what no labour can improve. In tragedy he is
always struggling after some occasion to be comick, but in
comedy he seems to repose or luxuriate, as in a mode of
thinking congenial to his nature. In his tragick scenes there is
always something wanting, but his comedy often surpasses
expectation or desire. His comedy pleases by the thoughts and
the language, and his tragedy for the greater part by incident
and action. His tragedy seems to be skill, his comedy to be
instinct.   (p. 112)

There are peculiarities in this judgment which on reflection might be adequately explained by recalling these three important elements in Johnson's make-up as a critic: his personal tendency to depression and melancholia; his training in neo-classical principles which he never fully outgrew; his views on language, particularly the use of conceits which he associated with 'metaphysical' poetry. His melancholia causes him to be repelled by the tragic view of life (of *Lear*: 'I know not whether I ever endured to read again the last scenes of the play till I undertook to revise them as editor') and so his claim that in tragedy Shakespeare 'often writes with great appearance of toil and study' is in effect an admission that his own reading of Shakespeare's tragedies is accompanied by toil and study whereas in the comedies he enjoys that exhilaration ('a mode of thinking congenial to his nature') which persuades him that comfortable reading must proceed from 'instinctual' writing. He preferred Shakespeare's comedies to his tragedies because he felt the need to be cheered up. He was aware of the sense of tragedy as a personal burden and did his utmost to hold it at bay. As a critic, Johnson felt more at ease with the comedies than with the tragedies because when he came to apply his theory of drama to the plays, a theory firmly rooted in neo-classical presuppositions, he found the comedies more amenable to his critical techniques and more suited to his taste. The personages are natural and therefore durable; they possess the uniform simplicity of primitive qualities, and above all, their 'mode of phraseology' is derived from the common intercourse of life, among those who speak only to be understood, without ambition of elegance. In tragedy on the other hand Shakespeare allowed himself to be seduced by 'some idle conceit, or contemptible equivocation'. Johnson's response to much of Shakespeare's high tragic style parallels his aversion from the 'metaphysical style' so roundly condemned in *The Life of Cowley*. Conceits and equivocations can only produce a comic effect and if they are used in tragedy the reader will gain the discomfiting impression that what should be tragic is trying to be comic, so the end result is frigidity.

Some of these ideas are expanded in that part of his essay which, following the pattern of previous editors, he devotes to a reasoned catalogue of Shakespeare's 'faults'. Most seriously, the principle of moral instruction is ignored. 'He seems to write without any moral purpose...he makes no just distribution of good or evil'. If anyone object that in so doing, Shakespeare is holding the mirror up to nature, Johnson might refer him back to *Rambler* no. 4: 'It is necessary to distinguish those parts of nature, which are most proper for imitation...It is therefore not a sufficient vindication of a character that it is drawn as it appears; for many characters ought never to be drawn.' If the author should find himself in a dilemma between his duty as instructor to his reader and his obligation to represent nature accurately, he should have no doubts about his choice.

Secondly, Shakespeare often ignores the principle of a unified plot. Sometimes he 'seems not always fully to comprehend his own design'. His 'catastrophe' is on occasion improbably produced or imperfectly represented. Thirdly, he lacks a historical sense; he is a 'violator of chronology'. Fourthly, he ignores the principle of social decorum. 'Neither his gentlemen nor his ladies have much delicacy, nor are sufficiently distinguished from his clowns by any appearance of refined manners.' Fifthly, in tragedy he labours overmuch and achieves only 'tumour, meanness, tediousness and obscurity'. Sixthly, in narration he affects pompous diction and a wearisome train of circumlocution. His declamations or set speeches are commonly cold and weak. 'Terrour and pity, as they are rising in the mind, are checked and blasted by sudden frigidity.'

Shakespeare is defended on the matter of infringing the unities of time and place; he has preserved the unity of action: 'His plan has commonly what Aristotle requires, a beginning, a middle and an end'. Arguments already used by Dryden, Howard and Farquhar are brought forward to justify Shakespeare's disregard of the unities of time and place. 'It is false that any representation is mistaken for reality; that any dramatick fable in its materiality was ever credible, or, for a single moment was ever credited.' Drama can only be credited, he says in a pregnant phrase, 'with all the credit due to drama'. Indeed, this is the source of our pleasure in drama: 'The delight of tragedy proceeds from our consciousness of fiction; if we thought murders and treasons real, they would please no more.' Verisimilitude, or the poet's truth to nature, demands consistency of characterisation and dialogue level with life, but stops short of insisting on 'true' murders. Imitations are to be preferred, not because they delude, but because they remind us of realities. This is particularly the case with comedy. Imperial tragedy, on the other hand, is always less powerful in the theatre than on the page. 'What voice or what gesture can hope to add dignity or force to the soliloquy of *Cato*?' Reading a play is as emotionally powerful as seeing it acted and it follows that, since the action is not supposed to be real, 'no more account of space or duration is to be taken by the auditor of a drama than by the reader of a narrative'.

Now it is time for the 'rules' to bow themselves out of English criticism:[10]

[10] Nichol Smith, *Eighteenth Century Essays.*

The result of my enquiries, in which it would be ludicrous to boast of impartiality, is, that the unities of time and place are not essential to a just drama, that though they may sometimes conduce to pleasure, they are always to be sacrificed to the nobler beauties of variety and instruction; and that a play, written with nice observation of critical rules, is to be contemplated as an elaborate curiosity, as the product of superfluous and ostentatious art, by which is shown, rather what is possible, than what is necessary.

He that, without diminution of any other excellence, shall preserve all the unities unbroken, deserves the like applause with the architect, who shall display all the orders of architecture in a citadel, without any deduction from its strength; but the principle beauty of a citadel is to exclude the enemy; and the greatest graces of a play, are to copy nature and instruct life. (pp. 121–2)

Johnson is aware that the old system with all its doctrine is no longer applicable to the present situation, nor can Shakespeare be pressed into conformity but the attempt to replace Aristotle by Shakespeare (as Farquhar suggested ought to be done) is equally unproductive. Johnson demonstrates that the old analytical tools are inadequate but he cannot be credited with providing feasible alternatives. Dramatic writing, it would seem, can now be defined as a skill which by describing accurately the emotional responses of its characters to the fictional situations in which they find themselves will provide pleasure through offering to the view of an audience a painless reminder of the kind of things that might happen to them. There is no idea of a literary or theatrical experience in its own right; there is only a literary description of other experiences, other emotions, offered in verbalised packages which can be interpreted by virtue of their close approximation to what we think or know the real experience to be like. This presumably is

143

what René Wellek means when he accuses Johnson of
having almost ceased to understand the nature of art
'and who, in central passages, treats art as life...He
paves the way for a view which makes art really superfluous, a mere vehicle for the communication of moral
or psychological truth'.[11] If the charge stands against
Johnson, it might equally be held against the entire body
of post-Renaissance critics in the field of dramatic poetry.
It is probably true that Johnson's real concern lay in the
direction of studying language as a means of com-
municating moral ideas and that his personal consciousness of guilt denied him the full enjoyment of that
disinterested objective and reflective pleasure which it is
the special province of poetry to provide. Thus his
reduction of neo-classical doctrine to the three principles
of moral instruction, pleasure through recognising the
imitation as being close to the thing itself and provision
of a storehouse of general statements about mankind
brought dramatic criticism in England to a temporary
halt. A new start had to be made and the jumping-off
point was already established in the general recognition
of Shakespeare's strength in presenting 'true-to-life'
characters. In the last quarter of the century the
approach to a new 'psychological' criticism is clearly
marked by such essays as Thomas Whateley's *Remarks
on Some of the Characters of Shakespeare* written about
1770 but not published till 1785; William Richardson's
*A Philosophical Analysis and Illustration of Some of
Shakespeare's Remarkable Characters* (1777) and Maurice
Morgann's *Essay on the Dramatic Character of Sir John
Falstaff* written in 1774 and published in 1777. From
these essays the line is clearly perceptible through
Coleridge and Hazlitt to Bradley.

[11] R. Wellek, *A History of Modern Criticism 1750–1950*, vol. I, p. 79.

# 6

## Diderot and Mercier

Denis Diderot (1713–84) is best known to the English-speaking world as the scholar who undertook a translation of Chambers's *Encyclopedia* into French. Under his hands this huge work of reference took on a life of its own and became a repository of advanced and frequently revolutionary thinking. In addition to his work as an encyclopedist, Diderot wrote prolifically on French life and culture, took up playmaking at which he never had any great success, and provided running commentaries on his plays which engage our attention because they indicate the new direction towards which European theatre is turning. The neo-classical theatre, the theatre of high tragedy and tragi-comedy, is nearing its end and is about to be replaced by a thoroughly bourgeois theatre concerned with middle-class lives and confronting middle-class problems. In England at this time Shakespeare is praised because his characters are so true to life, in many of their traits apparently so like ourselves, so close to 'nature' – meaning in this context human nature as experienced and interpreted by men of sound common sense. In like manner, Diderot demands of his theatre that it be so close to life that the spectator may imagine himself present at the action. The illusion of actuality must be as perfect as possible. Declamation, artifice, the grand style, are at all costs to be avoided because they will fail to move the audience and achieve that moral objective which is the aim of all artists – painters and poets, as well as playwrights.

## Neo-Classical Dramatic Criticism

Diderot's first essay in dramatic criticism lies interred in the middle of a tale written in the eastern romance tradition and entitled *Les Bijoux indiscrets* (*The Indiscreet Jewels*) (1748). This loosely articulated narrative form allowed room for lengthy asides, digressions and philosophical disquisitions presented at a popular level. (One may compare Johnson's *Rasselas* published ten years later.) It comes as no surprise therefore to find the principal character, an elegant lady of taste referred to as *la favorite* and pointing indirectly to Madame de Pompadour as her model, suddenly initiating a discussion on French classical drama:[1]

I don't understand the rules and even less do I understand the learned words in which they are conceived. But I do know that only truth pleases and moves. I know furthermore that the perfection of a play consists in such an exact imitation of an action that the spectator, deceived the whole time, imagines himself really present in the action. Now, in those tragedies that you boast about to us, is there anything that resembles that?

Her attendant replies that although these plays may be over-burdened with plot, this is a necessary evil. Diderot, speaking through madame, retaliates:

That's the final nonsense; unless we are to assume that it's not in the least absurd to fiddle merrily while our spirits are overwhelmed by the spectacle of a prince on the point of losing his mistress, his throne and his life... (p. 284)

Classical dialogue is castigated along with classical plots. Such plays are enveloped in pomp and tinsel so that they are remote from nature. The denouements are no better:[2]

---

[1] Quotations trans. from *Œuvres complètes de Diderot*, ed. Assezat, vol. IV, ch. 38.
[2] Diderot, *Œuvres*, vol. IV, ch. 38.

There are a hundred bad endings to one good one. You get the kind of denouement which is not adequately prepared for, or else miracles are summoned up. The writer becomes embarrassed by the presence of a character whom he has dragged through scene after scene for five acts, so he finishes him off with a knife thrust. The whole house dissolves in tears; as for me, I laugh hilariously. Then again, do people really speak in those declamatory tones? Do kings and princes in fact move quite differently from the manner of a man whose movements are natural? Do they really go around waving their arms, like folk possessed, like lunatics? When princesses speak, do they always utter a penetrating hiss? We are led to understand that we have brought tragedy to a high degree of perfection; as for me, I take it pretty well for granted that of all the categories of literature to which the Africans [sc. French] have applied themselves in recent times, tragedy is the most imperfect. (p. 285)

Encouraged by her entourage to continue the discussion, the favourite postulates the arrival of a foreigner in their country, who will be told that dreadful events are taking place in the court, some of which he may see if he looks through a peephole 'from where he can see the theatre which he takes to be the sultan's palace. Do you think that despite all the seriousness I can put on, the illusion would hold for this man for one moment?'

Selim, the attendant, gently insinuates into the discussion the notion that 'one surrenders oneself to the performance on the understanding that it is the imitation of an event and not the event itself which one is about to see' (p. 287). But the answer is given: need such an understanding prevent one from representing the occurrence in the most natural manner possible? The debate then tails off into a general comment on the state of letters in France, which 'might shine with more brilliance' if the authorities would start thinking along the new lines.

Cursory and tentative as these remarks were, Diderot was far from finished with drama and nine years later he offered to the world his own play, *The Natural Son*, hardly successful as a stage production but stolidly indicative of his desire to move the French theatre in a new direction. He looked to England for his models. Lillo's *The London Merchant* appealed to him through its honest attempt to move the passions with a tale of greed and murder set against a familiar middle-class background. Similarly Moore's *The Gamester* provided him with a pattern for this 'serious drama' which he felt must replace the old aristocratic and artificial tragic mode. In his own play however he was unable to move away from the sentiments and tone of the kind of drama he was busy condemning, and the result is an artificial love-honour-duty situation transferred awkwardly to the bourgeois drawing room.

Of special interest in the printed version is the elaborate machinery with which he surrounds the play for the purpose of establishing the reality of the situation and in so doing he anticipates in a peculiar manner Pirandello's *Six Characters In Search of An Author.* 'Vrai' and 'vrai-semblable' are being deliberately confused and the desires of 'la favorite' realised. He tells in his introduction how he meets a young man called Dorval who is the natural son in the play. Dorval says it was his father's great desire to have the dramatic crisis in their lives acted out, if only Dorval would script them. This he does and the events are re-enacted with all the original characters except the father who has in the meantime died, leaving the part to be played by a professional actor. Having read the play with little conviction that these verbose fictions could ever have been real people, we are invited to listen in to three discussions between Dorval and Diderot.

In the first discussion (*Œuvres*, vol. VII, pp. 87–101) we

learn that the three unities are hard to maintain but they are based on common sense. The playwright should not respect them overmuch nor should he throw them overboard without good reason. He must be guided by his sense of poetic invention. The art of plotting consists in tying events together so that the percipient spectator finds in them an acceptable rationale. Diderot, voicing the criticism of traditionalists, objects that Dorval talks in terms of familiarity with his valet and meets with the suitably Rousseauistic answer: 'Because they are our valets, have they therefore ceased to be men?' In the third discussion Diderot says he is against the introduction of servants at any point in the play: 'Honest people don't tell their business to their servants and if all the scenes take place between the masters, they will be that much more interesting.'

Now there comes a long discussion on the difference between a *tableau* – a set piece on the stage, each character establishing a visual relationship with the rest, as in a painting – and a *coup de théâtre*, a piece of melodramatic action which comes out of the blue and affects the characters in some way. The set piece is more true to life, characters are disposed in a natural and faithful manner. *The Natural Son*, however, is not devoid of *coups de théâtre* but, and here Dorval argues in the manner of Pirandello's 'father', they are there because that is the way the events took place. Art must be true to nature even when nature is melodramatic.

The second discussion (*Œuvres*, vol. III, pp. 102–33) begins with a consideration of the place of the spoken word in drama. Some of the lines of thought have been retraced in recent years by Antonin Artaud and his followers, particularly the general proposition that drama consists of much more than the recitation of words. Diderot calls for freedom for the actor to improvise, to express himself through gesture and pantomime and throw off the domination of the word. He should exploit those 'cries, inarticulate words, broken exclamations, monosyllables, mutterings between the teeth' (pp. 105–6) which can be so effective in appealing to the sensibilities of the audience. The spoken (scripted) word now appears to equate with the rational, the frigid and the moribund as opposed to the living passion generated by the actor's use of gesture. Thus, there are moments when the playwright must hand over to the actor:

Voice, tone, gesture, action, that's what belongs to the actor and that's what moves us, especially in the presentation of passion at its height. It's the actor who gives to the dialogue all its strength.   (p. 106)

Tirades, those long formalised emotional speeches of the seventeenth-century classical theatre are no longer viable in this new theatre where the words 'I love you' gain their effect from 'the trembling of the voice when they are spoken, the tears, the looks which accompany them' (p. 106). Gesture and intonation must work together, avoiding exaggeration, having no truck with the tirade, expressing genuine passion.

After some detailed discussion of matters illustrated by reference to *The Natural Son* the dialogue opens out on a general topic concerning modes of scenic presentation and how the emotions of the audience may be roused and their feelings so assailed that they will be almost afraid to go to the play and yet they will be unable to hold back. The Greeks could do this, says Dorval, and it could be done now, with a spacious stage which could be divided into two acting areas. Imagine Orestes in one, pleading at Minerva's feet for succour and the Furies in the other, determined on his extinction. The two areas merge into one. The Furies surround Orestes:

uttering cries, screaming with rage, waving their torches. What a moment of pity and terror that is, when one hears the prayer and the groans of the victim penetrate the cries and the terrifying movements of those cruel creatures who seek him out. Can we do nothing like this in our theatres? (p. 116)

This appeal to the Dionysiac spirit of drama comes oddly – at first sight – in the middle of a discussion on a domestically oriented play like *The Natural Son* until we recall that we are now in the second half of the eighteenth century and the seeds of Romanticism are beginning to germinate. No one, least of all Diderot, dares at this time write the kind of impassioned play that he seems to envisage. Some sixty years later Shelley completed *The Cenci*, a play of which one feels Diderot would have approved, and more than a century after that Artaud took up the same theme. One is not of course tracing influences here but there is at certain points an affinity between these three writers which if it does nothing else at least indicates how far Diderot had moved away from the age of Corneille and Racine. And now by making Dorval say, 'This discussion is taking us off the point' he changes the subject, almost conscious that the introduction of Orestes and the Furies may lead him into perilous country. The dialogue returns to a consideration of what is possible here and now, taking an ordinary domestic example and introducing the emotionally charged picture, a pantomimic passage, followed by a passage of speech which will consist mainly of a few monosyllables, an exclamation, a broken phrase. All this, says Dorval, is taking a route different from that so well trodden by Corneille, Racine, Voltaire and Crébillon, but this breakaway is essential if we are to free ourselves from the prejudices of the past. In short what is wanted is a new dramatic genre to be called domestic and bourgeois tragedy. The English already have it in Lillo's *London*

*Merchant* and Moore's *The Gamester*, both of them already
popular on the English stage for reasons which Diderot
strongly approved. Such a play, he goes on, must remain
true to nature, with genuine dress, genuine dialogue, a
simple and natural plot and no flamboyant dandies
uttering sesquipedalian words. This second discussion
ends with a further consideration of *The Natural Son*,
suggesting some amendments to the latter half of the
play which might have improved it. Diderot never
became reconciled to the fact that as a playwright he was
not a major success. Dorval expresses sympathy with the
proposed amendments but points out, in tune with this
new approach to dramatic realism, that 'then, it would
not be *our* story. And what would my father have said?'

The possibilities for a new kind of drama are further
considered in the third discussion. All drama, indeed all
art, it is roundly stated in good Scaligerian terms, has a
moral objective. It must be possible to draw a scale from
the extreme of tragedy to the extreme of comedy
through a middle range where men are not always
laughing or crying. This range we will call serious drama,
not to be confused with the *mélange* of high tragedy and
burlesque which the English incline towards. Since this
middle type of drama will lack the strong colours of the
extremes of tragedy and comedy, it will be necessary to
introduce every element which may add to its strength.
Thus, the subject must be important, the plot simple,
domestic and close to real life, with a powerful moral
vigorously stated and of general application.

The comic style is concerned with types and the tragic
with individuals:[3]

I mean the hero of a tragedy is such and such a man – Regulus,
Brutus, Cato, and no other. The principal character in comedy

[3] Diderot, *Œuvres*, vol. III.

{}

must on the other hand stand for a number of people... In serious drama (' drame sérieux') the characters will often be as typed as they are in comedy; they will always be less individualised than they are in tragedy... It is less the subject which makes a play comic, serious or tragic, than the tone, the passions, the characters or the central theme. The effects of love, jealousy, gambling, disorder, ambition, hatred, envy, may incite laughter, thoughtfulness or fear.  (pp. 138–40)

There are, in effect, no subjects which by their nature dictate their treatment, as in the old theatre where tragedy reigned in courts and comedy endured in cabins, where tragedy dealt with unique superhuman individuals and comedy with types. In this new theatre, treatment of the theme will be the dominant factor; even character will be less important, less individualised, more stereotyped because what matters is the situation, the environment, the interplay of passions in a setting which the audience will recognise as familiar and will thus the more readily imbibe the lesson, since the purpose of drama is 'to inspire the love of virtue and the horror of vice'.

A year after the *Discussion* on *The Natural Son*, Diderot addresses an essay in high-flown terms, reminiscent of his conversations with Rousseau, to his friend M. Grimm. In *Concerning Dramatic Poetry* (vol. VII, pp. 307–94) written in 1758 he enlarges on the idea of a dramatic scale ranging from comedy to tragedy and passing through intermediate stages of 'serious drama verging on the comic' to serious drama properly so-called (of which *The Natural Son* is an example) to 'serious drama verging on the tragic':

Here then is the sum of my dramatic system: gay comedy which is concerned with folly and vice; serious comedy which is concerned with virtue and duty; a form of tragedy which would be concerned with our domestic misfortunes and another form of tragedy which is about public catastrophes and the miseries of those in high places.   (p. 308)

He adumbrates the qualities of the poet who will be able to give us a vivid illustration of mankind's duties. Such a one must needs be a philosopher who will look into himself that he may see human nature. He must be deeply learned in the ways of society so that he may recognise its functions, its burdens, its advantages and disadvantages:

The duties of men are as rich a source for the dramatist as their follies and vices; honest and serious plays will succeed everywhere but where a people has become corrupt they will have even more meaning.   (p. 310)

The argument develops along his familiar line that when one writes, one must have in mind virtue and those who practise it. Theatregoers will learn to avoid the company of those wicked characters who confront them on the stage and will select those with whom they would like to share their lives. They will become reconciled to human-kind as it is, through seeing it portrayed on the stage:

Men of goodwill are rare but they exist. He who thinks otherwise accuses himself and shows how unlucky he is in having such a wife, such parents, such friends, such acquaintances.   (p. 310)

In short, everything that is, is good, including unsullied human nature. Miserable conventions pervert men but all men are moved by the story of a generous action. Where is the poor creature who can listen coldly to the complaint of an honest man? It is the dramatist's duty, Diderot suggests, to move sinners by putting in front of them a lifelike representation of honest men:

154

Oh what a deal of good would come to men if all the mimetic arts proposed one object in common, and one day came together with the law so as to make us love virtue and hate vice. (p. 313)

Having considered the purpose of drama to be in effect a kind of secular religion embracing beliefs about conduct, virtuous action and human relationships, Diderot turns to technics. Suspense, exposition, character, scenes, tone or social attitude, décor and dress (which should be simple and severe) each is considered in relation to his overall conception of drama, but from the point of view of the theorist rather than the man of the threatre who has to solve immediate practical problems. Least of all does he consider whether his ideas will be acceptable to an audience.

In chapter XXI, entitled 'Concerning Pantomime', he returns to his theory about the close relationship between stage presentation and the painted picture. He feels that at those very moments when actors should be free, creative, ready to improvise, they find themselves in the bondage of words. Gesture, he says, should often replace written text. 'There are whole scenes where it is far more natural for the characters to move around rather than speak' (p. 378). For this reason the plays of Plautus, Aristophanes and Terence are often misinterpreted because they give no clue as to the movements of their characters. In the domestic novel, and he cites Samuel Richardson here, it is the description of movement which delights as much as the dialogue. The very laws of pictorial composition can be applied to this aspect of visual stage presentation and they will be found identical in both cases. As the painter manipulates the placing of his figures on the canvas, so should there be a parallel kind of organisation on the stage. 'Pantomime is the picture which existed in the poet's imagination while he was writing' (p. 386). He concludes this section with the appeal:

Actors, enjoy your rights; do what the moment and your talent inspire you to do. If you are made of flesh and blood, things will go well without my interfering; and I'll interfere in vain, everything will go wrong, if you're made of marble and wood. (p. 386)

Here again, as in his plea for occasional outbursts of Dionysiac frenzy, he offers ideas which are ahead of his time. Prosaic as his own plays are, he genuinely recognises the need for a poetry of the theatre and this specific poetry will follow from a full appreciation of the view that drama is a representation of an action, expressed in visual terms, through patterned relationships seen on the stage, as well as in words. Actors must be allowed freedom to formulate these tableaux in whatever manner they think best. Their function is to act as well as to speak, to – in our modern training jargon – 'use space' rather than to concentrate on declamation.

Despite those insights, the essay as a whole, while being impressive in its intensity, enthusiasm and detail, is conceived in terms of the philosopher wearing none too comfortably the mask of the dramatist. His attempt to analyse the dramatist's craft from a formal and structural standpoint hardly conceals the bookishness in his writing. He insists that the man of genius needs no rules, or may ignore them all, yet he never ceases to advise his reader from a normative position, that this is bound to be better than that because the great end of drama is thus. Drama is for Diderot part of the total process of enlightenment through the reason and through the sentiments whereby ultimate good can at some time or other be achieved on this earth. The tenor of his frequent dialogues with

Rousseau emerges from this essay. Committed writing, soaked in moral awareness, exemplary, parabolic, leading readers and audience towards an understanding of the good, the true and the beautiful comprises for these philosophers a worthy item in the programme which they feel destined to carry through, a programme based on the urgent summons to social activity. If *The Natural Son* is a theatrical failure, he says, the fault lies not in the play but in the ignorance of the audience and the spite of the critics. Whatever mortal man can do to make drama part of the ultimate good has been done in this play. A real life situation has been expressed in theatrical, artifical, terms so that philosophical truths, hidden from the historian, are revealed to the sympathetic spectator. This is a prototype of the drama to come, the drama which will enlighten future generations, leading them away from a moribund concern with heroic displays to matters more immediate, more true and closer to nature. Diderot still rates Corneille, Racine and Molière as the major French dramatists but this is a style which suited yesterday. Tomorrow will reveal new paths which will lead towards the great ideal when men will learn to understand one another, to sympathise with one another, to make deliberate choice of the good even when confronted by the wicked, to be at one with nature, which is truth.

Some twelve years after the essay *On Dramatic Poetry* Diderot writes, again to his friend Grimm, a series of comments on the nature of drama with particular reference to the contribution of the actor. This piece of writing exists in two versions, the earlier being observations on his reading with obvious distaste a pamphlet entitled *Garrick or the English Actors.* Having sent his observations to Grimm, he re-wrote the essay in the form of a Socratic dialogue and entitled it *The Paradox of the Actor.* The final version was not published until 1830. The 'Observations' sent to Grimm sketch out the main argument which will be elaborated in the later *Paradox*. There is a distinct move away from the Rousseauistic position towards something more classical, more aware of the reflective objective nature of art. We must understand, he says, that the actor is not the character he portrays, he is only playing a part. Dorval can no longer leave the set and chat about his father's request to act the 'real' events. In playing his part, the actor is working with his head rather than his emotions. Actors with too much sensibility are limited in their art.[4]

The gladiator of old, like a great actor, and a great actor, like the gladiator of old, these do not die as one dies in bed; they must role-play another kind of death in order to please us.    (p. 350)

The actor must restrain his passions, keep a cool head, observe and discover through study and reflection everything which will achieve the biggest effect. Rehearsals may continue till the actors are worn-out and blasé. Only then will they begin to act well. He quotes with approval the story of an actress who reprimanded the stalls for giggling, then resumed her part of the grief-stricken woman. As a trained actress, she is capable of performing two different operations, the one expressing a genuine indignation at the behaviour of the audience, the other displaying her ability to intellectualise a simulacrum of grief.

The *Paradox of the Actor* continues the argument often in the same words:

I want an actor with judgment; he should be an onlooker, cool, calm; consequently I'm demanding penetration and certainly not anything in the shape of sensibility. I want him to demon-

---

[4]  Diderot, *Œuvres*, vol. VIII.

strate the art of imitating – or, what amounts to the same thing – an equal aptitude for all kinds of characters and roles. (p. 365)

The actor he has in mind is Garrick, with whom he had recently struck up an acquaintance. Ordinary people, he goes on, feel, but professional actors observe, study and depict. They are able, just as the dramatist is, to create a new world:

Great poets, fine actors and possibly in general all the great imitators of nature, wherever they may be, gifted with superb imagination, fine judgment, exquisite tact, genuine taste, are the men least endowed with sensibility. They are all too close to things, too busy watching, recognising, imitating, to be strongly moved within themselves. (p. 368)

You may think the great actor's talent consists in feeling but in fact it consists in showing the external signs of feeling with such minuteness that you are taken in. Everything the great actor does is premeditated, worked out, considered. Let the ordinary man put on the stage his familiar voice, his simple expression, his homely style, his natural gestures, and he will see what a miserable performer he is. Where do these great stage creations belong – Cleopatra, Agrippina, Cinna?

Put them in any social gathering and they would provoke peals of laughter. There would be whispered questions: Is he off his head? Where's this Don Quixote from? Where do you get tales like this? In what planet do people speak in this manner? (p. 370)

Fiction, in brief, is not fact. 'This formula was given by old Aeschylus: it's a protocol three thousand years old'. But Diderot's unnamed partner in the dialogue asks whether this protocol can last much longer. 'I don't know,' answers Diderot. 'All I know is that people seem to move away from it the nearer they get to their own age and country.'

Consider for a moment what is meant in the theatre by the phrase *être vrai*. Does this mean one presents things as they are in nature? Not at all. In that sense *le vrai* would mean only what is common to all. What then is *le vrai* on the stage? It is conformity of action, speech, face, voice, movement, gesture, with an ideal model imagined by the poet and often exaggerated by the actor...So it is that the actor in the street and the actor on the stage are two different people, so different you can hardly recognise them. (p. 373)

Diderot now moves on to a definition of the creative act which Wordsworth would have found acceptable:

When one is far removed from the crisis, when the spirit is calm...then memory conjoins with imagination, one recalling, the other elaborating the pleasure of a time that is past...If the tears flow, the pen falls from the hands; when you give yourself up to sentimentalising, then you stop composing...The sensitive man follows his natural impulses and the cry from his heart is the only true one; whenever he moderates or forces such a cry, it is not the sensitive man, it is the actor who is playing a part. (pp. 386–7)

Thus there is a clear distinction between nature and art. Nature is synonymous with sensibility and with truth. When sensibility is controlled, channelled, used as material for expression, the artist takes over. The actor as artist has the facility to reproduce all kinds of different 'natures' but he will not do this through exercising sensibility, or genuine feeling. At this point Diderot is led into a curious aside on the personal character of the actor whom he finds to be an empty soulless person and therefore little regarded in society. An actor who is a fine man, an actress who is an honest woman, these are rare phenomena. In general actors tend to be devoid of

160

background, breeding, culture and professional status. On the other hand, the actor as artist is something to be reckoned with in the hierarchy of creation. Expounding a scale of values faintly reminiscent of Plato and Sidney, he writes:

There are three models, the man created by nature, the man created by the poet, the man created by the actor. The natural man is less grand than that of the poet and the poet's creation is less grand than that of the great actor, who is the most exaggerated of the three.   (p. 419)

An audience is not moved by a display of passion:

People say an orator is the more powerful when he warms to his subject, when he works himself into a rage. I deny this. It's when he imitates a man in a rage. Actors impress the public, not when they are in a fury but when they are acting a fury…Passion itself is not effective; the imitation of passion is.   (p. 423)

Diderot has moved a long way from his search for a closer identification of nature with art, even to the point where he is anticipating the alienation effect of Brecht, wherein actors demonstrate an action rather than try to imitate it. He is discovering that there is a truth of nature and a truth of convention but they are not the same truth. The most truthful kind of drama is the most artificial. The honest actor is the actor who knows he is telling lies and who coolly reflects on the most efficient way of telling them. This is the paradox, to seek truth through an imitation of truth. The whole essay offers an example of Diderot in his character of the gifted amateur, the polymath voicing brilliant thoughts on virtually every subject known to his age – not excluding his father's craft of cutling on which he contributed a detailed article to the *Encyclopédie*. It would be idle to look for a comprehensive system in Diderot's ideas concerning the nature of drama and the actor's art. In his early days, under the influence of Rousseau, he is repelled by what he held to be the remoteness, the attempt to order and objectify experience through symbols, which he saw in the neo-classic dramatists. He recognised and rejected their courtly ancestry, preferring a theatre which was closer to the comic spirit than the tragic, but he was concerned that such a theatre should deal seriously with what he considered to be important issues in the lives of middle-class people, regarded not as heroic characters nor even as very unique individuals, but as types, categorised by trade and profession, of the new powerful bourgeois society. His two plays, *The Natural Son* and *The Father of the Family* were written to illustrate his specification for a viable new drama. Although he retained his admiration for his own plays to the end of his life, his later theorising indicates a radical revision of his views about drama and about art in general, a revision which could be broadly described as a return to classicism. The artificiality of art is not only recognised; it now takes a central position in his definition of art. Nature, that is, life at the diurnal material self-evident level, is one thing; art is another. They meet, not in the area of interpretation, of mimesis, because nature is no longer a safe guide (Samuel Johnson thought similarly when he objected to Shakespeare writing 'without any moral purpose...he makes no just distribution of good or evil') but rather in the field of moral intention: art is concerned with life in so far as it is the function of the artist to demonstrate and by implication approve of the morally sound life. It may be unwise for the artist to learn from nature; it would never be unwise for the audience to learn from the artist. The enlightenment has harnessed the theatre to its service and in return the actor will be elevated to a new station in society, a secular guide replacing the preacher in his pulpit.

About the time that Diderot was revising his ideas on nature, sensibility and verisimilitude, a younger writer, Louis Sebastien Mercier (1740–1814) published a *New Essay on the Art of Drama* which went far beyond Diderot in declaring that the theatre must become 'like the drum that will one day waken the dead...a simple and luminous rhetoric should in a moment rouse a nation asleep' (Introductory *Epistle to his Brother*). Mercier, a dedicated writer and follower of the radical philosophical movement, even to the point of being known as 'Rousseau's monkey', had written several plays with little success until the seventh, *Natalie,* was produced by the Comédie Française in August 1773. Anger at his comments on actors in the *New Essay* closed the doors of the Comédie on him, and his plays lay unacted for over a decade until they were taken up by the Italian company housed in the new *Boulevard du Temple.* Despite Lanson's dismissal of Mercier in a one-line footnote (*Histoire de la littérature française*) the essay is worth closer examination. The basic doctrine behind it is plain Rousseauism. Man is born good; man can be led back to goodness; the purpose of drama is to help to lead man back to goodness. 'The theatre is an illusion' he says in his introduction:[5]

it must be brought into accord with the profoundest truths: the theatre is a representation; such representation must be given a purpose, must be put at the disposal of the greatest number so that the images it offers may bring men together in the overpowering emotions of compassion and pity. It's not enough that the spirit be kept busy, or even moved; it must be led towards the good. The moral aim, without being either con-

[5] Quotations translated from Mercier, *Du Théâtre ou nouvel essai sur l'art dramatique*, 1773

cealed or made too obvious, must take hold of the heart and establish its rule there.

The theatre must correct those who have the wrong views about life, develop the understanding of the unintelligent, and teach vacillating men those things which they need to hate, to love and to value. Good theatre is contemporary theatre. Let kings sleep in their ancient tombs. Mingle the pathos of tragedy with the charm of comic realism. The theatre teaches in a different way from that of the moral philosopher. The man who cannot be moved in the theatre is a scoundrel. In his second chapter Mercier attacks the Greek and Roman theatre with every conceivable argument – a theatre of dreams, oracles, warnings and fatalism and old irrelevant legends. The neo-classical theatre is synthetic, false, bizarre, unintelligible. Plautus is dirty. Even Corneille and Racine are not spared, although he had written ten years earlier: 'What pleasure to rise to the heights with Corneille, weep with Racine and laugh with Molière.'

What is real tragedy about? he asks in chapter two of the *Essay*. Real tragedy will concern all citizens, will be in touch with current politics, will unfold to the people their true interests, encourage an enlightened patriotism and love of country.

That is genuine tragedy, which has hardly been known except among the Greeks and which can make its voice heard with pride only in a land where the voice of liberty has not been stifled. In any other context, there will be nothing but a picture lacking substance, or sometimes a kind of adulation disguised in fine language. This will neither interest nor enlighten me because it will in no way respond to the secret vices which I have within myself...

What study is more worthy of a poet than to be fully aware of what he should reveal to his age at the instant he is writing and

164

thus to fit his drama to the circumstances of the day so that abuses may be at one blow revealed, attacked and if possible, put right; to know how to work on public opinion; to give it timely warning against some hateful law. ...He will teach his audience to recognise the roads to despotism.   (ch. 2)

In short, the dramatist must be commentator, teacher, ombudsman and even legislator. To him who would argue that the lives of kings are of more interest than those of ordinary folk, Mercier answers: 'Only as they are men, not as they are kings'. Tragedy becomes a menace when it lends a kind of grandeur to the activities of criminals, e.g. Nero, Narcissus, Cleopatra, Atreus, Mahomet. French classical tragedy indoctrinated the people with the idea that to be a good citizen one must be a good slave. The Greek idea of fatality 'a yoke under which mortal man must stoop' is obnoxious, replacing courage by despair, justifying atrocities and vengeance. We see an innocent and virtuous Oedipus delivered over to the horrors of incest and the remorse of a parricide. Nothing is to be learned from history. 'Only the philosopher can study history, for others it is a source of error...the reading of Tacitus produced a Machiavelli.' (ch. 3)

On comedy, which he discusses in the fourth chapter of the *Essay*, Mercier has equally strong moral views. Comic writers should not merely attack foibles for the purpose of raising an empty laugh.

I think it is more necessary to be concerned with an attack on vice which is more dangerous than foibles and possibly more susceptible to correction. In effect what happens is that an outdated piece of idiocy is nearly always replaced by a current piece of idiocy and often you cure one only to contract the other, which may be even more tedious. Wouldn't a dramatist be wiser and wouldn't he be fulfilling the function he has taken on himself more adequately if he were to direct all his efforts against vice, pursuing it even into the shadows and boldly unmasking it. The virtuous man – this is well known – often behaves ridiculously while the vicious man who is more cunning gets off scot-free through concealing his actions. (ch. 4)

Comedy should be a serious act of correction rather than a lighthearted reflection of innocent absurdities. Comedy and laughter are not necessarily synonymous. Even Molière fails – except in *Tartuffe* – to wage war on vice:

In profoundly admiring Molière, I do not hesitate to blame him…He has taught our youth to mock their parents, to scorn the old and make a joke of their infirmities; he has dared to put adultery on the stage and make the stalls his accomplice. (ch. 7)

Having dealt with classical tragedy and comedy, he turns in chapter eight to an examination of the new genre, the 'drame':

I am going to prove that the new sort of play called 'Drame' which combines tragedy and comedy, having the pathos of the one and the simple outlines of the other, is infinitely more useful, more true, more interesting, as being more within the grasp of the mass of the citizens…

I am a man, so I cry to the dramatist, show me what I am! Reveal to me my faculties! It's your job to interest me, to instruct me, to move me. Up to now, have you done so? Where are the fruits of your work? Why have you laboured? Have your successes been confirmed by popular approval? Maybe the people don't even know of your existence, or your work. So what influence has your art had on your age or your compatriots? (ch. 8)

The answers to his questions lie in the word 'drame'. It was a sad day for art when tragedy and comedy became separated, so that tragedians felt in honour bound to

166

make their audiences weep and comedians to make them laugh. The early tragi-comedy was a failure,

because the mixture went to extremes and became absurd. Transitions were too rapid and so put the audience off. Courtly characters were set up against the yokels. The low, not the familiar, ruined the serious business and there was none of that unity which is not only an Aristotelian rule but a rule of good sense. This genre was in its essence good but became unacceptable in practice, smothered under a load of productions which discredited it. (ch. 8)

He moves on to a definition of 'le drame', a genre which will be both interesting and moral:

Drama can provide an interesting spectacle because all sorts and conditions of men will be part of it. Likewise it can present a moral spectacle because moral uprightness can and should dictate its laws. (ch. 9)

This kind of spectacle will pillory vice and so call down justifiable ridicule upon it. Laughter will be present too because virtue will emerge triumphant after some setbacks. Such a theatre will reflect its own age 'for the characters, virtues and vices will be essentially those of this day and this country'. Comedy is a different kind from this for comedy lacks scenes of pathos, of nobility, scenes offering moral lessons. 'Le drame' must be serious, must not derive solely from the actions of one character, must avoid the novelettish, must seize on those actions which conform to truth. An honest artisan is better material for drama than a marquis. In drama there is no enforced, extreme over-zealous action: rather the dramatist will seize a beautiful moment in human life, a moment which reveals the secrets of a family. The details will be there along with the broad significant features.

The dramatist's choice of subject is Mercier's next

concern. The poet might journey to Lyons, Marseilles, Bordeaux, Nantes or La Rochelle to depict the distinctive characteristics of the inhabitants and the regions, this to be done in such a manner as would correct their failings and highlight their good qualities; even to England, Spain and Russia, and then we would have universal understanding and harmony. The frivolous voluptuary, the prodigal paying for his folly, the atheist, the charlatan, the political adventurer, these should be our targets. 'My pen falters when I think of all the monsters in our society – the vicious, the cowardly and the dishonourable.' And again, (note on p. 115 of the *Essay*) 'I believe in God, in his wisdom, in his goodness, in a system which declares that all is for the best.' 'I believe in everything which honours, elevates, aggrandises human nature.' (note, p. 116) When the law has forgotten to punish, the dramatist must reform. Nothing stirs the audience more than a scene which arouses pity. Surely the misfortunes that fall on ordinary folk are no less important than the misfortunes of other men. The poet is the public orator of the oppressed. His task is to make the proud, however hardened they are, hear their groans and listen to the thunderous voice of truth.

In chapter twelve Mercier withdraws for a moment from his obsession with content and considers style, structure and technics. Nature is not to be slavishly imitated:

It is not enough merely to imitate nature; one must select those objects and features which are to be imitated. Such imitations must not be a frigid and slavish copy but a wise and enlightened picture which will draw a veil over deformity and make visible only what will add to the total coherent effect of the picture. 'Le drame', it cannot be too often repeated, is the representation, the picture of bourgeois life in all its facets, gay, sad, sentimental or moral. Is a drama to be nothing but a novel in dialogue form?

Is it enough to strive for a moral end only to provide a picture of complicated and extraordinary adventures. To what end? What's the good of it? (note, p. 140)

The representation of nature and of character does not mean detailed naturalism as in Italy where forty people are needed on the stage to represent a crowd and one sees a man get out of his carriage, sit at table, eat, drink, take coffee – all very true, but inept. Action should be *vraisemblable*, credible, and to ensure this the laws of possibility, place, time, customs of society and of individuals, are guide lines but not inviolable. The one essential unity is the unity of interest. Any drama where the main interest is divided will be an imperfect work.

How does the poet set about his task? How does he prepare himself; what are his sources of experience? Some people might say that this is pretty simple stuff, an easy refuge for mediocre scribblers:

Who won't be able to write a drama? A drama in prose? Who indeed? Anyone, who might be able to produce a good enough tragedy. But it's not enough to have learned Corneille, Racine, Voltaire and Crébillon by heart, to take on the spirit of imitation, to steal their hemistiches, to copy their full exact rhymes. Our kind of poet must have studied the world and men and their characters. The hand of experience must be brought to bear on the customs and subterfuges of civil polity. The proprieties must be long and deeply considered and fully understood. It is not possible to ignore these practical details, these *entr'actes* in human life, which, holding the big scenes together, give the real picture of the social round. You need the sure touch of the *philosophe* to mix the simple and the familiar with the sublime, to bring comedy and pathos together without blurring the fine edges of either and without setting them at variance and so making them shocking. (ch. 15)

The dramatist must needs go, not to books, but to the financier, the shopkeeper, the artist's studio and among the humblest people. He must know his milieu, the weaknesses, faults and virtues of men whom he observes as he walks among them. Hospitals and hovels, fêtes, ceremonies, churches, places of entertainment and even the scaffold should be his resorts. He must know the common people and work for them, for without their approval he will achieve nothing. As an ironical comment to this excellent advice, one may note in passing that Mercier never succeeded in writing a really good play but he did come up between 1781 and 1788 with a massive fourteen volume study, *Le Tableau de Paris* which described the society, customs, sights and character of his native city.

The *Essay* concludes with a few random broadsides against critics past and present, Aristotle, Horace and D'Aubignac being singled out among the famous. He might have been wiser to have laid his pen down after the twenty-third chapter since smaller men than Aristotle or Horace, and men still living, took umbrage at his carping. In particular, the doors of the Comédie Francaise were closed against him. His commentary on Aristotle amounts to little. Given his prejudices, one would hardly expect him to be in sympathy with the Greek. He explains catharsis in terms which satisfy his preconceptions about the function of drama. Quoting the phrase: 'The theatre purges the passions while exciting them' he writes:

Either this phrase is an absurdity or it can be explained thus: the only passions which need to be mended are vicious passions. Now the only way they can be mended is by strengthening our pity and compassion; by cultivating this moral and interior sense which warns us of what is noble and just, which rouses our indignation against wickedness, which causes our tears to flow on behalf of adversity. (ch. 24)

The comment is accompanied by a footnote invoking pity: 'sweet and generous sentiment of pity! noble emotion! happy thrill of a sensitive soul! be perfect in man! as long as he recognises you, he will never be wicked.' To such simplicities were the prophets of the enlightenment able to reduce human nature. Elaborate theorising and schemes are anathema to Mercier since they detract from the directness and clarity of his conception of drama as being a moral fable appealing to everyone, denouncing evil, defending the cause of the oppressed and educating opinion. Comparing Aristotle, Horace and Diderot, he prefers Diderot although even he tends to overdo his praise of the dead and so denigrates the living. His closing comments on the rhetoric of drama are consistent with his general theories in their support of prose against verse. 'Since it is men who are speaking, drama must be presented in the garb which becomes it...the best lines in verse drama are the simple prosaic ones.' Like Scaliger, Mercier believed that the theatre was a medium for the telling of exemplary stories which would nurture moral excellence in the individual citizen and so induce harmony and well being in the state.

Inspired by Joseph Saurin's successful adaptation of Moore's *The Gamester* for the French stage in 1767, Mercier took up Lillo's *The London Merchant* and turned it into a different kind of play, which bears just enough resemblance to the original to make comparison a useful exercise in highlighting the differences between the English and the French interpretations of bourgeois drama. Where the English play is tough, calvinistic and calculated to appeal to a puritanical merchant audience which regularly encouraged its revival through the middle years of the century (179 performances between 1731 and 1776) the French version, entitled *Jenneval* and virtually re-written round the same group of characters, concentrates on the mind and emotions of the young anti-hero, treats him sympathetically and by invoking some last-minute melodramatic action, prevents the murder and permits everyone to accept the entire series of incidents as a didactic chapter in the growth of a young man.[6]

Mercier explains his purpose in a lengthy *Preface* wherein the general theories expressed in the *New Essay on the Art of Drama* are given a practical application:[7]

I wanted to depict the sad consequences of a vicious liaison, to make passion appear as terrifying as it is dangerous, to rouse aversion for those delightful and despicable women whose trade is seduction, to demonstrate to impetuous and imprudent youth that crime is never far from debauchery and that in drink a man will ignore the extremity of his fury.  (p. 3)

Thus far his thinking is akin to that of Lillo, who writes in his *Dedication* to Sir John Eyles:[8]

Plays founded on moral tales in private life may be of admirable use by carrying conviction to the mind with such irresistible force as to engage all the faculties and powers of the soul in the case of virtue by stifling vice in its first principles.  (p. 4)

The manner of presenting the moral lesson must however be adjusted to the French taste for refinement. Mercier goes on:

We take pity on weakness, misfortune, even tempestuous passions, but we have no tears to spare for a murderer. His purposes are foreign to us. He is no longer a member of society. His crime weighs on our spirit, overburdens us; nothing

---

[6] Jean Hamard in *Revenue de littérature comparée* (1965, vol. 39, pp. 589–604) compares Lillo, Mercier and an Italian version by G. de Gamerra.

[7] Quotations trans. from *Théâtre complet de M. Mercier*, Amsterdam, 1778, vol. 1.

[8] Lillo, *The London Merchant*, ed. McBurney, Regents' Restoration Drama Series, E. Arnold, 1965.

justifies it, nothing excuses it in our sight, and the Paris theatre cannot come to terms with such enormity.

But how to preserve the dramatic energy of the play and at the same time have regard to that French delicacy which in this connection seems to be right and proper? How to depict passion in all its force without losing sight of the moral purpose, to induce a shudder without horror? I have led the young man to the edge of the abyss. I have caused him to calculate its depth. It would have been easy for me to have thrown him down. But I appeal to the nation. Could an audience, without paling fearfully, have watched a lunatic led on by the thirst for gold and lechery rush to sink a dagger in the heart of a man of virtue? No, they would reject the scene because it is not meant for them and they do not admit the existence of a parricide in their midst, these sensitive souls who come to be moved and to weep at the spectacle. One may be moved, alarmed, without the poet wringing one's heart miserably and uncomfortably. Is it necessary to hurt in order to cure? Is it not enough to engulf the soul in the sweet sentiment of pity, this all-conquering sentiment which enwraps us and which gains a victory both gentle and intimate? Can one credit that this weak and misguided young man will never be able to see the light and free himself from this spell without our having to thrust in front of him, in the theatre, the rope, the gallows and the hangman? And why may we not, in this touching and terrible situation, where a woman's voice demands a murder, why may we not permit this tortured confused youth a return to virtue? Is not such a return natural and does not this fresh moral purpose which such a return implies, by providing a noble conception of the victorious forces we conceal within ourselves, does not this give satisfaction to public and philosopher alike? (pp. 4–6)

The consequence of all this, not unnaturally, is that he finds he has to write a new play. He takes the original situation of wicked woman encouraging simple young man to murder innocent uncle for money, but transfers it to the Paris of his own day, concentrating attention on the chaotic state of the youth's emotions and allowing the idea of murder to germinate not only through the seductress's prompting, but also as the development of an angry confrontation with his hard-headed unsympathetic relative. Significantly, Jenneval himself is not called on to do the murder. This will be carried out by a professional thug who is foiled at the last moment by the repentant young man. Despite his earlier connivance at his uncle's death, Jenneval is in the closing scene lauded as something of a misguided hero and amid general tears carries off the hand of the fair Lucile. Mercier's handling of the action, when compared with Lillo's, amply illustrates the new direction which serious drama is trying to take. There is a strong commitment both to society and to the unique worth of the individual who is represented as a plain man repulsing the forces of evil which lie within himself and winning because he eventually allows the forces of good to control him. While George Barnwell is a domestic Faustus of the old school, condemned to learn that the wages of sin is death, Jenneval is the new man designed by Rousseau and ready to beget a long lineage of Romantic heroes.

Mercier concludes the *Preface* to *Jenneval* by some general comments on what he considers to be the drama of the future. Most playwrights up till now have written for only a handful of men but now they must write for the ear of all the people. Even Corneille has become something of a stranger. We are no longer concerned with matters of great moment but with ordinary folk. Nearly all writers have despised the work of countryfolk or have seen in them nothing but coarseness, but the time is ripe for the shepherd to take the stage and the monarch to step down. There now follows an interesting reversal of Castelvetro's theory of the 'difficulté vaincue'. Castelvetro argued that the play should exhibit the marvellous but this had still to be presented within the bounds of verisimilitude, so the more successful the playwright was in solving this paradox, the more honour was due to him. Mercier claims contrariwise that the old tragedy is so remote from normal human affairs that no one knows (or presumably cares) whether the events are true but the new dramatist will find his themes in the real and immediate misfortunes of people like ourselves and such plays will be difficult to write because everyone can check on the resemblance and so they must be accurate or the effect will be totally lost. Finally, he repeats his plea that the dramatist, having cast off the shackles of aristocratic tragedy, should not confine himself to portraying only the middle classes of society:

The poet who can portray for me the poverty-stricken labourer, surrounded by his wife and children, toiling from dawn to dusk, unable to escape the horror of the misery which wears him down, will present me with a truthful picture, one which I have right in front of my eyes. Such a picture given to the nation should enlighten it through sympathy, give it healthier ideas about politics and laws, show the evils of these as they are now, and in consequence be more useful than the narration of distant revolutions taking place in states which never at any time come close to us.   (p. 8)

Mercier is a suitable figure with which to conclude the main part of this essay for he looks back to the neo-classical past and forward to the Romantic future. In his concern with form – he considers *The London Merchant* confused and chaotic in its structure, which it is – he is thoroughly French and neo-classical. His faith in the audience's, or indeed to use his own favourite word, the nation's readiness to learn from plays relates him to Scaligerian authoritarianism and to eighteenth-century rationalism. His belief in man's capacity to improve himself – even to attain some stage close to heavenly

175

perfection on earth – and his demand that dramatists write about and for ordinary people (the poet, said Wordsworth, 'is a man speaking to men'), place him firmly among the early Romantics. His plays are hardly masterpieces – reading him makes one sympathise with Artaud's attack on the proliferation of words in the theatre – but his vision as a critic and commentator on the scene around him is not to be despised.

# 7

## Conclusion

It took about a hundred years for the visions of Diderot and Mercier to be realised. By the end of the nineteenth century the Freie Bühne in Berlin, the Théâtre Libre in Paris, the Independent Stage Society in London, were offering to minority audiences that kind of thought-provoking drama which the critics of the enlightenment felt to be its proper province, a drama which concerned itself with its relationship to real life, to society, to morality. A further move in the direction of naturalism, foreseen by Mercier and encouraged by the novelists of the later nineteenth century, introduced the idea that ugliness, being an aspect of nature, must have access to the stage. Plays might be unpleasant as well as pleasant. Unpleasant plays admitted that virtue was not always triumphant nor vice cast down. In this respect the move towards naturalism helped to resolve the eighteenth-century dilemma that in following nature, drama might be led into portraying actions which were neither elevating nor instructive. The argument now stated that a confrontation with the ugliness of nature (i.e. society) moved men in the direction of improvement. To meet with ugliness was the first step towards eliminating it.

Despite these new developments, the fundamental nature of the play had changed little. We still, at this time, have a theatre which describes, a mimetic theatre, a theatre devoted to the telling of stories about men and women who might almost have lived in reality, but who are the more interesting because they have a fictional life which can be revealed to us in all its secret complexity. This theatre knows its place in society, knows how to set about its business, how to reveal to its audience what has happened before the curtain rose, how to lead them up a series of emotional heights and down the other side and satisfy them with a well-told tale. This is a theatre which assumes that a tale can and should be told well, and told in a rational manner because, by and large, it reflects a rational universe. So a refined process of formal shaping is relevant, involving acts and intervals, cause and effect, introduction and development, psychological conflict, plot and characterisation, those attributes of the drama which the neo-classical critics accepted as self-evident, because they were clear in their own minds that the theatre had a prescribed form and a defined purpose. Between the sixteenth and the twentieth centuries, this form and this purpose suffered only minor adjustments. The concept of verisimilitude as reflecting a general truth about nature became narrower so that mimesis took the shape of a mirror image of life as it is or is assumed to be. As to its purpose, long held to embrace the two-fold aim of providing delight and instruction, drama kept pace with the demands of the new democratic thinking and undertook the obligation to remind society of its duties towards all its members, not only those whom fortune favoured. Despite these changes, the old assumptions are still there, that men and their condition can be improved, that they are rational beings, that given inducement in the shape of an exemplary tale they can be encouraged to take thought and solve problems. Even now, in the latter half of the twentieth century, the majority of west-end successes and television plays, other than the obvious farces, vaudevilles and idle pastimes, adhere more or less closely to the traditional form and purpose with which we have become acquainted through the specimens in this book.

## Conclusion

This traditional theatre is of course now under heavy fire. The first attack can be traced back to that extraordinary collection of writings by Antonin Artaud published under the title *The Theater and Its Double*. Artaud's strategy was to undermine what he held to be the Aristotelian basis of the established theatre, a theatre which concentrated on character studies of dead people.[1]

If people are out of the habit of going to the theater, if we have all finally come to think of theater as an inferior art, a means of popular distraction, and to use it as an outlet for our worst instincts, it is because we have learned too well what the theater has been, namely, falsehood and illusion. It is because we have been accustomed for four hundred years, that is, since the Renaissance, to a purely descriptive and narrative theater – storytelling psychology; it is because every possible ingenuity has been exerted in bringing to life on the stage plausible but detached beings, with the spectacle on one side, the public on the other – and because the public is no longer shown anything but the mirror of itself...And I think both the theater and we ourselves have had enough of psychology.   (pp. 76–7)

Artaud accuses Aristotle of binding the theatre to psychological imagery. Psychology must be replaced by metaphysics:[2]

In other terms, the theater must pursue by all its means a reassertion not only of all the aspects of the objective and descriptive external world, but of the internal world, that is, of man considered metaphysically. It is only thus, we believe, that we shall be able to speak again in the theater about the rights of the imagination.   (p. 92)

The reduction of Artaud's argument to its essentials – by no means an easy task for it is part of his rhetorical tactic to throw words around like fire-bombs – would seem to

---

[1] Antonin Artaud, *The Theater and Its Double*, trans. M. C. Richards, Grove Press, 1958.
[2] Ibid.

lead to the conclusion that what he is pleading for is a new poetry of the theatre. Psychology for him is a descriptive science, deadening in its precision, having only a cerebral appeal. This is the state of the traditional theatre, exact, stereotyped, intellectual, lifeless. What is needed is a language, not composed of words, which will act directly on the senses, nerves, emotions and sub-conscious levels of the audience's apprehension. The predictabilities of plot, the prescribed lineaments of characterisation are to be confounded or ignored. Such propositions might be condemned as leading only to the cul-de-sac of a new and decadent romanticism, an art theatre for 'in' people and there are already several of these flourishing in the cultural centres of the western world. But this will hardly do as a final word on the possibilities of a new drama. Artaud is surely right when he senses that the traditional form of the theatre, which has existed for four hundred years and which, as we have seen, can be analysed in terms adopted from neo-classical critical procedures, is ceasing to be the comprehensive medium it once was and is ripe for re-assessment, if not, sooner or later, total extinction.

Until recently, attempts to 'bring poetry back' to the theatre have looked like a series of forced injections, with the patient squirming at the painful unnaturalness of the operation. Poetry, we have discovered, if we did not already know, is not like paint. It cannot be used as a coating on a prose play. Artaud suggests that the search for a poetry of the theatre through words alone will be vain. Both on and off the stage it has become the fashion to suspect words. Eugène Ionesco has made this suspicion one of the cornerstones of his tragic-comic method although in each succeeding play he seems to increase his reliance on the logic of statement. Samuel Beckett appears to have waged a lifelong battle with words and, after a run of verbose novels, eventually caught the public imagination with a play remarkable for its economy, its poetic overtones and its successful defiance of the traditional 'rules' of structure. Both Ionesco and Beckett are conscious of the twentieth-century retreat from rationality. The form and purpose of life itself are no longer as precise, as definable as they once were and this uncertainty is reflected in the serious drama of our time. Artaud sensed this breakdown of an ordered universe and sought what he felt to be a more honest art form in the primitive, the non-intellectual, the feverishly emotive. Beckett has moved to the opposite pole and writes a kind of drama which is cold, shrivelled, loveless and impoverished – a dramatic rendering of total nihilism which in the long run can be appreciated only as an intellectual game hardly relieved by the turns of wit and moments of pathos in some of the dialogue. In his plays, the delight is pale and the instruction negative.

It may be that we live in times when the zest, the robustness, the emotional intensity which have vitalised the greatest drama at all periods are smothered by alien anxieties about material welfare, the horror of death or the uncertainties of life. Even the drama critic finds that he is repeatedly asking himself what he is looking for in the theatre. The certainties of the seventeenth century are gone for ever. And yet one wonders whether the neo-classical critics in their combined wisdom did not ask most of the fundamental questions about the nature of drama, while we are still groping for the answers.

# Select bibliography

Addison, J. *The Spectator with Sketches of the Lives of the Authors*, Edinburgh, 1802

Anderson, M. *The Essence of Tragedy and other Footnotes and Papers*, Washington, 1939

Aristotle, *Poetics*, Loeb Classical Library, Heinemann, 1965

Arnaud, C. *Les Théories dramatiques au* XVII*ᵉ siècle*, Paris, 1888

Artaud, A. *The Theater and Its Double*, trans. M. C. Richards, Grove Press, 1958.

Auerbach, E. *Mimesis*, Princeton, 1953

Boswell, J. *Life of Samuel Johnson*, ed. Ingpen, Bayntun and Bath, 1925

Bredvold, L. I. *The Intellectual Milieu of John Dryden*, Ann Arbor Paperbacks, Michigan U.P., 1966

Brereton, G. *French Tragic Drama in the 16th and 17th centuries*, Methuen, 1973

Burns, E. ' *Theatricality* ', Longmans, 1972

Castelvetro, L. *La poetica d'Aristotele vulgarizzata et sposta*, Basle, 1576

Chapelain, J. *Opuscules critiques*, introd. A. C. Hunter, Librairie Droz, Paris, 1936

Corneille, P. *Œuvres complètes*, ed. M. Ch. Marty-Laveaux, Hachette, Paris, 1857

Dacier, A. *La Poétique d'Aristote avec des remarques critiques*, Paris 1692

Daiches, D. *Critical Approaches to Literature*, Longmans, 1964

D'Aubignac, F. *La Pratique du théâtre*, Amsterdam, 1715

Diderot, D. *Œuvres complètes de Diderot*, ed. A. Garniers, Paris, 1875

Dryden, J. *Dramatic Essays*, J. M. Dent (Everyman) London, 1912

# Select Bibliography

Elledge, S. (ed.) *Eighteenth Century Critical Essays*, Cornell U.P., 1961

Frye, N. *Anatomy of Criticism*, Princeton U.P., 1957

Gassner, J. *European Theories of Drama*, ed. B. H. Clark, New York, 1964

Gosson, S. *The School of Abuse*, English Reprints, Murray, 1868

Harth, P. *Contexts of Dryden's Thought*, Chicago U.P., 1968

Horace, *The Epistles and De Arte Poetica*, ed. Wilkins, Macmillan, 1889

Hume, R. D. *Dryden's Criticism*, Cornell U.P., 1970

Johnson, S. *Lives of the English Poets*, ed. G. Birbeck Hill, 3 vols. Oxford, 1905

Jonson, B. *Complete Works*, ed. C. H. Herford, P. and E. Simpson, Oxford, 1925–52

King, B. (ed.) *Dryden's Mind and Art*, Oliver and Boyd, Edinburgh, 1969

Lawton, H. W. *Handbook of French Renaissance Dramatic Theory*, Manchester U.P., 1949

Mélèse, P. *Le Théâtre et le public à Paris sous Louis XIV 1659–1715*, Librairie Droz, Paris, 1934

Mercier, L. S. *Du Théâtre ou nouvel essai sur l'art dramatique*, Amsterdam, E. van Harrevelt, 1773

Olson, E. (ed.) *Aristotle's Poetics and English Literature*, Gemini, 1965

Rapin, R. *Réflexions sur la Poétique d'Aristote*, Paris, 1674

Scaliger, J. C. *Poetices Libri Septem*, Heidelberg, 1617

Sidney, P. *An apology for Poetry and other works*, ed. Feuillerat, C.U.P., 1912

Smith, D. Nichol (ed.) *Eighteenth Century Essays on Shakespeare*, O.U.P., 1963

Spingarn, J. E. (ed.) *Critical Essays of the Seventeenth Century*, Indiana U.P., 1963

Styan, J. L. *The Elements of Drama*, C.U.P., 1960

Swedenborg, H. T. (ed.) *Essential Articles for the Study of Dryden*, Frank Cass & Co., 1966

Ward, C. E. *The Life of Jn. Dryden*, N. Carolina U.P., 1961

Wellek, R. *A History of Modern Criticism 1750–1950*, Cape, 1955

Wilson, A. M. *Diderot*, O.U.P., 1972

# INDEX

Academy, French: Chapelain's relations with, 51, 53; examination of *Le Cid*, 53

action: imitation of, 5; Scaliger on, 23–6; Castelvetro on, 30; Corneille on, 70, 74, 75, 78; Dacier on, 91; Dryden, through Lisideius, comments on unity of, 97

actor: seldom mentioned in early criticism, 6; Diderot on the, 150, 155, 157–61

Addison, J., against 'poetical justice', 126

Aeschylus: *Agamemnon*, 78; Rapin on, 81

anagnorisis, 11

Archer, W., 62, 76

Aristophanes, Diderot refers to, 155

Aristotle: misinterpreted, 2; and social function, 4; *The Poetics*, 7–13; tentative approach, 16; Scaliger on, 20, 21; Castelvetro on, 30; Sidney on, 38; Jonson on, 45, 47; Chapelain on, 53, 54; D'Aubignac on, 58, 61, 65; Corneille on, 67, 68, 69, 70, 71, 73, 74, 77, 78; Rapin on, 81, 82, 83; Dacier on, 86–9; French critics on, 92; Howard on, 101; Dryden on, 106–8, 114; Dennis on, 118; Farquhar on, 120, 122, 123; Rowe on, 127; Pope contrasts A. and Shakespeare, 130; Johnson compares them, 142; attempts to replace A. by Shakespeare, 143; Mercier attacks

him, 170; compares him with Diderot, 171; Artaud attacks, 179

Arnaud, C., 66

Artaud, A., 149, 151; *The Theater and its Double*, **179–80**

audience, 44, 55, 67, 68, 76, 104, 116, 122, 135, 143; Scaliger on, 21; Castelvetro on, 30, 31, 33; D'Aubignac on, 61, 63; fears for itself, 71; ladies in the, 84; Elizabethan, 130, 131; changes in, 137; Diderot on, 150, 155, 161, 162

Auerbach, E., 100

Barrault, J.-L., 67

Beckett, S., **180–1**

Boswell, J., 7

Bradley, A. C., 8, 144

Brecht, B., 161

Bredvold, L. I., 95

Castelvetro, L., 3, **27–33**, 49, 58, 62, 125; Sidney's reading of, 39; Corneille quotes, 70; Dacier on, 86

catharsis: Aristotle on, 8; Minturno on, 18; Scaliger on, 20, 21; Corneille on, 69, 72, 73, 79; Rapin on, 80, 81; Dacier on, 87, 92, 93; Mercier on, 170

Chapelain, J., **51–5**, 92, 115

character: Aristotle on, 5, 8; Scaliger on, 22–6; Corneille on, 69, 70, 76; Shakespearean compared with Greek, 106; unheroic, 112; relation to action, 123; Diderot on, 155

185

# Index

chorus, 6; Horace's view, 15; Scaliger on, 21; Jonson unsure about, 43–4; should be brought back, 86; Dennis on, 117

Cicero, 26

Coleridge, S. T., 144

Collier, J., *A Short View of the Immorality and Profaneness of the English Stage*, 113

comedy, 43, 45, 128; metres suited to, 15; is pleasanter, 18; differs from tragedy, 19; Castelvetro on, 30, 31; Sidney's definition, 37, 40, 41; D'Aubignac defines, 64; Corneille on, 69, 76; Dacier on, 91; mixed with tragedy, 97; rhyme not essential in, 99; Howard on, 101; Farquhar on, 121; Johnson on, 134, 140, 142; Mercier's views, 165–6

Corneille, P., **66–80**, 81, 92, 93, 97, 106, 107, 109, 151; *Le Cid*, 51, 53, 54, 55, 72, 73, 74, 78; Chapelain reports on *Le Cid*, 51–5; D'Aubignac refers to, 65; *Le Menteur*, 70; *Théodore*, 74; *Nicomède*, 76; *Pompée*, 78; Dacier challenges, 87, 88, 89, 90; Dryden influenced by, 96; Diderot's estimate of, 157; Mercier on, 164, 169

Dacier, A., **85–92**, 135, 137; Dennis on, 116, 117, 118

Daiches, D., 96 (and n)

D'Aubignac, l'Abbé, 6, 67, 74, 79, 86, 92, 170; *La Pratique du théâtre*, **57–66**

delight, *see* pleasure

Dennis, J., **117–20**, 122; *The Impartial Critic*, 117

denouement, 77, 86, 147

*deus ex machina*, 77

dialogue, 15, 100, 107, 138, 142; Diderot's views on, 150

diction, 5, 12, 69, 71

Diderot, D., 2, 3, 4, 6, 94, **145–62**, 171, 177; *The Natural Son*, 148–53; *Les Bijoux indiscrets*, 146–7; *The Paradox of the Actor*, 157–61

Donatus, 6, 20, 96

Dryden, J., 42, 48, **95–113**, 117, 118, 122, 123, 128, 142; *An Essay of Dramatic Poesy*, 96–100, 110; *Defence of an Essay of Dramatic Poesy*, 102–6, 110; *Observation on Rymer's Remarks on the Tragedies of the Last Age*, 106–8; *The Grounds of Criticism in Tragedy*, 108–10, 112; *Preface to 'An Evening's Love'*, 110; *The Indian Emperor*, 110; *Defence of the Epilogue to the Second Part of 'The Conquest of Granada'*, 110; *Prologue to 'Aurung-Zebe'*, 111; *Preface to 'All for Love'*, 111; *Dedication of 'The Aeneas'*, 113; Pope compared with, 131; *Aurung-Zebe*, 133

Eliot, T. S., 96, 99

Erasmus, 19

Euripides, 81, 107, 114; *Cyclops*, 50, 57; *The Suppliants*, 78

farce, 41, 64, 101

Farquhar, G., 142, 143; *A Discourse upon Comedy*, 120–3

Fletcher, J., 99, 106, 109, 110

Freie Bühne, Die, 177

*Gammer Gurton's Needle*, 41

Garrick, D., 7, 159

*Gorboduc*, 37

Gosson, S., 43; *The School of abuse*, 35

*hamartia*, 12; Dacier's treatment of, 90

Hardy, A., 50

Harth, P., 95 (and n)

Harvey, G., 35

# Index

Hazlitt, W., 144

Hédelin, F., *see* D'Aubignac

Heinsius, D., 47, 48, 58, 61, 120

hero, 134; Aristotle's definition of the tragic, 11–12; Scaliger on, 20; Castelvetro on, 28; Corneille examines Aristotle's definition, 71–2; Dryden on, 109, 112

Horace, 4, 8, 20, 26, 39, 43, 44, 48, 58, 78, 120, 136, 170, 171; *Letter to the Pisos* (or *The Art of Poetry*), 13–16

Howard, Sir Robert, 122, 142; *Preface to Four New Plays*, 100; *Preface to the 'Duke of Lerma'*, 100–2

humanism, 32

Hume, R. D., 95 (and n)

Ibsen, H., *The Wild Duck*, 9

illusion, 163, 179; maintenance of, 49, 51; D'Aubignac's views on, 60; Dryden on, 103; Diderot on, 147

imitation, 79, 87, 168; poetry the art of, 36; Chapelain on, 51, 55; Corneille on, 78; poetry not a direct i. (Dryden's discussion), 99, 103; Pope on, 129; Johnson's view, 135, 141; Diderot on, 146, 147, 161

Independent Stage Society, 177

instruction, 86, 116, 122, 178; Horace on, 15; Chapelain on, 55; Corneille on utility or i., 68–9; Dryden on, 107; theatre a centre of, 113; in Johnson's *Preface*, 139, 141, 143

Ionesco, E., 180

Johnson, S., 7, 8, 56, 126, **132–44**, 162; *Rambler*, 132–5, 141; *The Idler*, 135; *Preface to Shakespeare*, 136–44; *Life of Cowley*, 141; *Rasselas*, 146

Jonson, B., 16, 37, 41, **42–8**, 65, 99, 104, 109, 116, 131; *Prologue*

to 'Everyman in His Humour', 42–3; *Address to the Readers of 'Sejanus'*, 43; *Volpone*, 45–6; *Discoveries*, 46, 47; *The Alchemist*, 47; *Bartholomew Fair*, 51; *The Silent Woman*, Dryden's criticism of, 98

justice, poetical, 12, 91, 107, 115, 125; Rymer's use of the phrase, 114

Ker, W. P., 111

Lanson, G., 163

Laudun, P. de, 49

Le Bossu, 109, 111; *Le Traité du poème épique*, 87

Lillo, G., 174; *The London Merchant*, 148, 151; Mercier's adaptation of, 171, 175

Machiavelli, *The Prince*, 34

marvellous, the, 123, 174; Castelvetro on, 31, 33; Chapelain on, 54, 55

Menander, 15

Mercier, L. S., 4, 5, 77, **163–75**, 177; *New Essay on the Art of Drama*, 163–71; *Preface to 'Jenneval'*, 172–5

mimesis: Aristotelian usages, 1, 5, 10, 162, 178; Scaliger reinterprets, 22; rhyme or blank verse in connection with, 99; Dryden discusses, 103

Minturno, A., 18–19, 81

Molière, 64, 157, 164, 166; *Le Misanthrope*, 92

Moore, E., *The Gamester*, 148, 152, 171

Morgann, M., 124, 144

naturalism, 5, 56, 81, 112, 169, 177; Corneille's theory reflects move towards, 77; Dryden senses the move, 113; encouraged by Collier, 113

187

# Index

necessity, 92; in Aristotle, 10; Corneille on, 74–5; a fundamental law (Johnson), 134

Ogier, F., 49–50
Olson, E., 12

pantomime, 155
Pirandello, L., *Six Characters in Search of an Author*, 148
pity and fear (or terror): in Aristotle, 8, 12; Robertello and Minturno on, 18; Corneille's explanation, 71–4, 79; Rapin on, 82–3, 85; Dacier on, 88, 89, 93; Dryden on, 106, 107, 108; Johnson on, 133, 142
Plato, 47, 72, 87, 161; Sidney refers to, 36
Plautus, 48, 61, 64, 164; Sidney refers to, 38, 40; Diderot refers to, 155
pleasure, 46, 50, 54, 67, 68, 82, 83, 85, 86, 89, 93, 135, 139, 143, 147, 178; Horace on, 15; Castelvetro gives primacy to, 28, 29, 32, 33, 34; Sidney on, 36, 40; Chapelain says not enough in itself, 52, 53; Dryden's view, 102; derived from our consciousness of the fiction (Johnson), 141
plot, 6, 53, 102, 121, 146, 152; Aristotle on, 8–9; Rymer on, 114, 116; Shakespeare not good at (Rowe), 127; same from Johnson, 141; Artaud against, 180
Plutarch, 127
Pope, A., 116, 138; *Preface to Shakespeare*, 129–31
probability, 104, 123; Aristotle on, 10; Chapelain's concern with, 53–4; Corneille's treatment of, 74–6, 78, 92; Rymer's emphasis on, 114, 115
Pyrrhonist, 95

Quintilian, 26

Racine, 151, 157, 164, 169
Rapin, R., 93, 94, 96, 114; *Réflexions sur la Poétique d'Aristote*, 80–5; influence on Dryden, 108, 110
Richardson, S., 155
Richardson, W., *A Philosophical Analysis and Illustration of Some of Shakespeare's Remarkable Characters*, 144
Richelieu, Cardinal, 51, 53, 57
Rivandeau, André de, 49
Robertello, F., 17, 18, 70, 72
*Roderick Random*, 133
Romanticism, 151
Rousseau, J. J., 153, 157, 162
Rowe, N., *Some Account of the Life etc. of Mr. William Shakespeare*, 126–9
Rymer, T., 12, 91, 96, 118, 120, 139; Dryden writes observations on *Remarks on The Tragedies of the Last Age*, 106–8; translates Rapin's *Reflections*, 114; *Tragedies of the Last Age*, 114–15; *A Short View of Tragedy*, 115–17; Dennis replies, 117

Scaliger, J. C., 1, 2, 6, 29, 41, 47, 58, 94, 96, 120, 136; *Seven Essays on Poetry*, **19–27**; ideas well-known in France, 49; D'Aubignac follows, 63; Mercier's affinity with, 171
Saurin, J., adapts *The Gamester*, 171
scene, 21, 78, 98, 155
scepticism, 95
Scudéry, Chapelain replies to, 53, 54
Seneca, 10, 38, 47
sensibility, 91, 163; too much bad for actors (Diderot), 158; to be controlled, 160

# Index